Diana
Princess of Wales

A biography by
PENNY JUNOR

Sidgwick & Jackson
London

FOR JAMES AND PAM
with thanks

First published in 1982 by
Sidgwick & Jackson Limited
First paperback edition 1983
Second paperback edition 1984
Copyright © Penny Junor 1982

ISBN 0-450-5579-5

Typeset by Robcroft Ltd
Printed by Collins, Glasgow
for Sidgwick & Jackson Limited
1 Tavistock Chambers, Bloomsbury Way
London WC1A 2SG

CONTENTS

LIST OF ILLUSTRATIONS AND PICTURE
ACKNOWLEDGEMENTS

FOREWORD

WHEN I FIRST began my research for this book, I contacted Buckingham Palace, who said they could be of no help. The Princess was too young to have a biography written about her, they said, and, besides, there were too many other people doing the same thing.

Four months later, after foot-slogging around the countryside, visiting all the places Diana had lived in her life and the schools that she had attended, knocking on doors, talking to friends and relations who have known her and people who have worked for her family, following the royal couple round Wales, and never once coming across anyone else involved in writing a book about her, I went back to Buckingham Palace to suggest that, out of all those biographers they had told me about, I was the only one trying to do any original research.

At this point there was a change of heart, and I do thank Michael Shea, the Queen's Press Secretary, for his subsequent help. He persuaded Diana to answer a long list of questions I put to her, and he read painstakingly through the manuscript, checking facts and weeding out errors. Information about the early years, which only Diana's immediate family could verify, has also been checked and corrected, and I am very grateful to everyone involved.

But my greatest debt is to all the people closest to Diana whom I cannot name, but who spoke to me about her, in some cases putting their friendships in jeopardy in the interest of helping me to produce an accurate picture of the Princess – to offset so many inaccurate stories that have gone to print in the past. Without their trust, and the help of those who persuaded them to talk, I could never have begun the task of writing this biography.

January 1983   P.J.J.

INTRODUCTION

HOW, YOU MIGHT wonder, do you write a biography of someone who is just twenty-one years old and who has spent nineteen of those years in almost total obscurity? The answer is, with great difficulty. I have had to scour the length and breadth of the British Isles – wearing down a set of car tyres and very nearly the author too – to find people who were willing to talk about Diana. But it has been surprisingly worthwhile.

Diana has done nothing remarkable in her life – her most notable achievement is marrying the heir to the Throne – but the bizarre things that happened around her in those early years, and the ways she learnt to cope with them, help to explain the person she is today and to understand why she has made such an impact on the public, how she has managed to turn the Establishment on its head, and why she is likely to have so much influence as Princess of Wales.

If she hadn't inherited class or wealth, with her lack of qualifications she would be lucky to get a job selling ice-creams in a cinema. As it is, she is the most famous, most photographed and most talked-about woman in the world, and in all probability will one day be Queen.

Screeds have already been written about Diana, and you might well question whether there could have been anything else left to write. All I can say is that there was; and it was quite a revelation to discover, amongst all those screeds, just how many inaccuracies and downright fabrications have been printed about her in the past. One of the biggest obstacles that I came across, in fact, in persuading people to talk to me about her was their fear of being misquoted again.

The gushers have turned Diana into a paragon, which she never was. She isn't fluent in French, a brilliant dancer, the highlight of the ski slopes or the mainstay of the hockey team.

1

She isn't even always very good with children. The cynics have said she is a very pretty clothes-horse, but as thick as two short planks. She isn't that either. She is no intellectual, but she is far from stupid. Diana is a born survivor. There is a strong will behind that pretty face, but such charm, and genuine charm, that people do exactly what she wants – Prince Charles included – without ever realizing that they didn't think of the idea themselves.

Anyone else who had come through the childhood that she has experienced might have gone off the rails long ago. Certainly few twenty-one-year-olds could have survived so well the last three years: the cameras, the crowds, and the inability to go anywhere or do anything alone or without being recognized and watched. There may be Rolls-Royces and palaces, but hers is not a job most people would wish on their worst enemy.

Diana's strength is that she regards herself first and foremost as a wife. Her ambition as Princess of Wales is 'being a good wife'. Most girls become a 'Mrs' when they marry; she became a princess, but for no better reason than the man with whom she fell in love happened to be a prince. She wears the jewels and the clothes – even the crown – with great relish, but underneath them all she is still her old self, and behaves in exactly the same way she has behaved all her life. People have always had to accept Diana on her own terms, and they still do.

THE ROYAL CONNECTION.

IF ANYONE had suggested the name Lady Diana Spencer as a bride for the Prince of Wales three years ago, the response would have been 'Lady Diana Who?' Even those people who have made a profession of marrying him off would have dismissed the idea as ridiculous. She was the eighteen-year-old sister of one of Charles's ex-girlfriends, and in every other respect totally unknown.

Today, as Princess of Wales, she is possibly the most famous woman in the world and, single-handed, she has reawakened an interest in and a devotion to the monarchy which haven't been seen in years.

In retrospect, however, she was the perfect choice in every way. Indeed she is far better suited to the role she will have to play as Princess of Wales than she could ever have been had she been a royal.

Her family has been close to the Royal Family for generations, as friends as well as servants. This generation is no exception. The Queen, the Queen Mother and the Duke of Kent are godparents to Diana's two sisters and brother, while her father's godparents were Queen Mary and the Prince of Wales who became Edward VIII. Earl Spencer served as equerry to George VI and to Elizabeth II; his mother, Countess Spencer, was a Lady in Waiting to the Queen Mother, and Diana's maternal grandmother, Ruth, Lady Fermoy, still occupies that post. And so it has been throughout the centuries.

Lady Diana Spencer came from the very top drawer of British aristocracy: she can trace her ancestors through as much, if not more, blue blood than Prince Charles himself. They are, in fact, related – both are descendants of Henry VII and James I – and, depending upon which common ancestor you take, are sixteenth cousins once removed, eleventh cousins once removed, or seventh cousins once removed – via William Cavendish, the 3rd Duke of Devonshire. They are also related through Charles II and his brother James II – five lines lead back to Charles's innumerable children born the wrong side of the blanket, and one to an illegitimate daughter of James II and Arabella Churchill, sister of the 1st Duke of Marlborough.

But the fact that Diana is a member of the aristocracy and not a member of the Royal Family makes all the difference. She has had a normal childhood. She has queued for a bus, run to catch a train, stood at a supermarket check-out, ridden a bicycle through the traffic, jostled with the crowds in the January Sales. Yet though she knows how ordinary people live she has always led a privileged life, make no mistake. Mummy seldom doubled up as cook, dishwasher, bedmaker and chauffeur in her early days, and there were never problems of noisy neighbours through the walls at Park House. But she has seen how the other half lives in a way that no member of the Royal Family ever could. As a result, she knows how to talk to people, she knows instinctively what will please them, and has a genuine ability to communicate.

However, because Diana was born into a family whose lives have been entwined with those of the Royal Family for generations, she has never had cause or opportunity to question the protocol of royalty. She understands about discretion and duty, and she takes for granted the pomp and ceremony. At the same time, if the Queen had called at Park House for a drink during a weekend at Sandringham, she would have been no more awe-inspiring than any other grown-up friend of the family might have been. And, off duty, the ways in which both families spent their time were really very similar.

So, when asked some time before her engagement to Charles whether being in the company of the Royal Family made her feel nervous, it was not surprising that Diana replied: 'No, of course not! Why should it?' As her father said later, 'The average family wouldn't know what hit them if their daughter married the future King. . . . But some of my family go back to the Saxons – so that sort of thing's not a bit new to me. . . . Diana had to marry somebody, and I've known and worked for the Queen since Diana was a baby.'

Earl Spencer wasn't actually working for the Queen when Diana was born. He had given up his job as equerry when he had married Diana's mother in 1954, and by the time Diana was born he was farming. But the family lived in a house rented from the Queen on the Sandringham estate, just a few hundred yards from the main house, and when the Royal Family were there for their annual holiday in the New Year, they would meet.

Diana was born the Honourable Diana Spencer. Her father Edward John, known as Johnnie, was then Viscount Althorp – he only inherited the title of Earl Spencer when his father died in 1975. Diana's mother had been the Honourable Frances Ruth Burke Roche before she married, the younger daughter of the late 4th Baron Fermoy, and of Ruth, Lady Fermoy.

Diana was born at Park House on 1 July 1961, the couple's fourth child. Her appearance was both a relief and a disappointment, for they already had two daughters, Sarah, then six, and Jane, four, and were not-so-secretly hoping she would be a boy. Their third child had been a boy, born eighteen months previously, but he had died just ten hours later. It had been a double tragedy for the Althorps. As with all titled and landed families, they felt it was imperative to produce a male heir. They had lost not just a baby, but a male baby, and they would have to keep trying until they got another.

But Diana was clearly going to live, and even if she was the wrong sex, which at first left them with no ideas about a name for her, they were undoubtedly delighted with the new arrival. Nearly three years later Frances finally did give birth to a boy, Charles, who is now Viscount Althorp, and the all-important question of succession was taken care of.

While Diana was still a toddler, she and Prince Charles are said to have first met. Charles's teenage head was not turned by this plump, golden-haired, neighbour in nappies, and neither of them can remember the incident at all – but she more than made up for this when next they met.

A link between Spencer women and royal princes is something of a tradition, and Diana was not the first Diana Spencer to have turned the head of a Prince of Wales. But she was to be the first to marry one, and make their match respectable. Four of her ancestors were mistresses to English kings in the seventeenth century, three to Charles II, and one to James II. But perhaps more scandalous was Georgiana, the daughter of Diana's great-great-great-grandfather, the 1st Earl Spencer, whose life and loves were the talk of the entire nation in the eighteenth century.

Georgiana had married at seventeen the 5th Duke of Devonshire, a man whom she referred to as the Dog, and to whom she was immediately and repeatedly unfaithful. One of her lovers was the portly Prince of Wales, who later became George IV, and who was never certain, when she became pregnant, whether she was carrying his child or not. He certainly visited her throughout the confinement with such paternal interest that he even, it was said, 'excited some emotion' in her husband the Duke. And the Prince kept letters from her, which so shocked George V when he discovered them a hundred and thirty years later, that he burned the lot.

Georgiana, known as the Duchess of Dimples, and 'the face without a frown', went on to have other passionate affairs, including one with the Whig Charles Grey, who was seven years her junior. Meanwhile her sister, Henrietta, who became Lady Bessborough, caught the eye of the same Prince of Wales twenty-four years later. By that time the once merely portly Prince was no pretty sight. As Henrietta wrote to her ex-lover, Lord Granville, in 1809: 'Such a scene I never went through. . . . After another long tirade, threw himself on his knees, and clasping me round, kissed my neck before I was aware. . . . He continued, something struggling with me, sometimes sobbing and crying. . . . Vows of eternal love, entreaties, and promises of what he would do – he would break with Mrs Fitzherbert and Lady Hertford, I should *make my own terms*! . . . That immense grotesque figure flouncing about half on the couch, half on the ground . . . '. She resisted his charms, and one Spencer woman's honour remained intact, from her royal suitor at least.

But while Spencer women frolicked with kings and princes, Spencer men became courtiers, and Althorp, which has been in the Spencer family since the early sixteenth century, must have had more royal visitors over the years than almost any other private house in England.

The Althorp estate in Northamptonshire was originally leased from the Abbot of Evesham in 1486 by John Spencer, and not bought until 1506. The house's appearance in those days was very different from the way it looks now. Originally it was a moated red-brick building with a central courtyard. John Spencer's grandson, Sir John, added the forecourt wings in 1573, and his great-great-great-grandson's widow, Lady Dorothy Sidney, enclosed the courtyard and turned it into a grand saloon with a wide wooden staircase leading to a picture gallery above, which is still there in all its glory today. The present Earl Spencer remembers Diana scooting down those stairs on a tea tray.

Lady Dorothy's son, Robert, who was the 2nd Earl of Sunderland, improved the house and the park further, so that by 1675 the diarist John Evelyn could write of the house:

It is placed in a pretty open bottom, very finely watered and flanked with stately woods and groves in a park with a canal. The house, a kind of modern building, of freestone, within most nobly furnished; the apartments very commodious, a gallery and noble hall. It was moated round after the old manner, but it is now dry and turfed with a beautiful carpet. Above all, are admirable and magnificent the several ample gardens, furnished with the choicest fruit and exquisitely kept. Great plenty of oranges and other curiosities.

The house remained very much like this until 1786 when George, the 2nd Earl Spencer, commissioned the architect John Holland, who had designed Carlton House for the Prince Regent, and Brooks's Club in St James's, to remodel Althorp. It was he who clad the red-brick exterior with white tiles baked in Ipswich, which were fashionable at the time, and rearranged the interior, bringing the state rooms from the first floor down to the ground floor, where they are today.

But in the early days Althorp was nothing more than a

second home. Most of the year the Spencer family lived at the manor house at Wormleighton in Warwickshire. The family was fabulously rich, having amassed great wealth from sheep farming. The first Lord Spencer, great-great-grandson of the man who bought Althorp, owned nineteen thousand sheep, and at the accession of James I in 1603 he was said to have more ready money than any other man in England. Nothing in those times impressed royalty quite like cash. Spencer was sent by the King as Ambassador to Württemberg to present Duke Frederick with the Order of the Garter, and had a promising career ahead of him, but working at court didn't impress him. He was far happier at home managing his estates, and no doubt counting his sheep.

Although he actually spent more time at Wormleighton his son William, who became the second Lord Spencer, was born at Althorp. He in time built a racecourse in the grounds, and established the Easter race meetings on Harlestone Heath nearby. His son, Henry, the eldest of ten children, became as reluctant a courtier as his grandfather had been. He inherited the title at sixteen, the same year that he went to Oxford. Just six years later, in 1642, civil war broke out and Henry joined the Royalists against Cromwell and his Parliamentarian rebels. Charles I rewarded him for his loyalty, and for his loan of £10,000 towards the cause, by creating him Earl of Sunderland in June 1643. A few months later he was killed in battle, at the age of twenty-three, leaving a widow and four young children.

This marked the end of the house at Wormleighton too. Soon after Henry's death, Prince Rupert spent a night at the manor house before the Battle of Edgehill and, after leaving it, Royalist troops burned the house to the ground to prevent it becoming a garrison for Cromwell's forces.

Thereafter the Spencers lived at Althorp. Henry's widow, who had been Lady Dorothy Sidney (the 'Sacharissa' of Edmund Waller's poems), brought up their four children there. The eldest, Robert, who became the 2nd Earl of Sunderland on his father's death, grew into a brilliant if devious and unscrupulous politician, fired by his perpetual need of money to pay for extravagant rebuilding at Althorp

8

and his compulsive gambling. Althorp had become 'almost a gambling house' in his time there. He made himself indispensable to three kings: Charles II, James II and William III; and flirted with whichever religion, either Catholicism or Protestantism, was likely to do him more good at the time. In the 1670s he became Ambassador in Paris, Madrid and Cologne, and used his time abroad to collect pictures and furniture from all over Europe which he brought home to embellish Althorp so that, according to John Evelyn, the rooms were 'such as may become a prince'. By 1682 he had become Secretary of State, and was later Lord President of the Council, Lord Chamberlain, a Lord of Regency, and the first Spencer Knight of the Garter.

But when James II's Queen unexpectedly gave birth to a son – so suddenly that a legend arose that the baby had been smuggled into her bed in a warming pan – Sunderland found that he had backed the wrong horse. He announced his conversion to Rome but at that late stage it did him no good – he was dismissed from office in 1688 and fled to Holland, where he acquired himself some Van Dycks and a few other Dutch Masters, and ostentatiously attended the Protestant church. This last ploy was to make up to William of Orange who had landed in England a month before he fled, and was now King William III. The stratagem worked and in 1690 Sunderland was back at Althorp again; three years later he was installed as William's chief political advisor.

His next task was to try to marry his son Charles to Anne Churchill, the younger daughter of John Churchill, the great Duke of Marlborough, and of the redoubtable Sarah. This proved something of a problem, for the Spencer finances were still uncertain and it was no secret that Charles held some dangerously extreme political views. He had become a violent, doctrinaire Whig and, according to Jonathan Swift, 'would often, among his friends, refuse the title of Lord, swear he would never be called otherwise than Charles Spencer and hoped to see the day when there should not be a peer in England'.

It was as well for the twentieth-century Spencers that Charles was restrained, and that Anne went ahead with the marriage in 1699, because it is through that marriage that the present family have the house, the title and some of the fabulous treasures.

Anne, after giving birth to five children, had a premonition that she was going to die young, and instructed her husband that her mother, Sarah, should bring up any of the children who were still young enough to need care. As it happened, she didn't die until she was thirty-two, by which time three of her surviving children were capable of standing on their own two feet. But the youngest, Diana, was only six, and she was duly taken in and brought up by the famous and formidable Duchess Sarah.

The present-day Diana, coincidentally, was also six when her mother left home; her mother was thirty-two; and it was her maternal grandmother who took Diana under her wing and, in her daughter's absence, helped to rear her grandchild. Moreover, a great many people believe that Diana's match with Prince Charles was largely engineered by their grandmothers.

Back in the 1730s Duchess Sarah, who doted on her 'dearest Di', her 'Cordelia', also hatched a plan to marry her favourite grandchild to the Prince of Wales, although she was less successful. He was Frederick, Prince of Wales, eldest son of George II, newly arrived from Hanover, and in debt. A day was fixed, so the story goes, for them to be married secretly at the Duchess's Lodge in the Great Park at Windsor, and Sarah was to part with a dowry of £100,000 for Diana. But their plot was sabotaged by the Prime Minister, Sir Robert Walpole, who had come to hear of it and had other plans for the Prince of Wales. The following year Frederick was married to Princess Augusta of Saxe-Gotha in St James's Palace. In the circumstances, Diana was probably better off. The Prince of Wales can't have been such a dazzling catch if he is remembered for nothing better than his epitaph: 'Poor Fred, who was alive and is dead'. Instead she married Lord John Russell and later became the Duchess of Bedford.

Even after her marriage to John, Diana, whose first child died at birth, continued to see a great deal of her grandmother. If distance separated them, they wrote to each other two or three times a week. Sadly Diana didn't live long, but before she died, in the autumn of 1735, she believed that she was pregnant once again, and Sarah advised her accordingly. In a letter dated 15 July:

I think there can be no doubt of your being with child, but perhaps not so long as you reckon. I hope you will continue to drink but very little wine; for I have reason to think that is a right method from several accounts I have heard of women that miscarried till they tried that way of drinking a great deal of water and sometimes milk. My Lady Portland says that it is an admirable thing to take every morning as soon as you wake a glass of spring water. And I have known some do it at night when they go to sleep.

Diana was suffering terrible sickness and didn't appear to be growing any bigger. Sarah dealt with this in a letter dated 17 August: 'It is not natural for any great bigness to appear in four months, when a person is very tall and very lean.'

Her last piece of advice was written a week later: 'Though I remember when I was within three months of my reckoning, I could never endure to wear any bodice at all; but wore a warm waistcoat wrapped about me like a man's and tied my petticoats on the top of it. And from that time never went abroad but with a long black scarf to hide me. I was so prodigious big.'

Her advice was to no avail. Diana died of galloping consumption a month later on 27 September, and it is doubtful whether she had ever actually been pregnant at all.

Duchess Sarah had had no sons, so when her husband, the 1st Duke of Marlborough, died in 1722 her grandson Charles, Diana's eldest brother, had inherited Blenheim Palace and the Marlborough title, thus dividing the Spencer family. This meant that when Diana's father died it was his second son, John, who inherited Althorp and the Spencer estates. But the Marlborough branch of the family also kept the name Spencer until 1817 when Charles's grandson, the 5th Duke, took the additional surname of Churchill by royal licence.

Sarah didn't care at all for her eldest grandson, Charles, but she was very fond of John; and when her 'dearest Di' died, John became the principal legatee in Sarah's will. This explains why so many of Sarah's personal possessions and treasures – paintings, china and exquisite pieces of furniture – are today at Althorp and not at Blenheim Palace.

John Spencer also died young, at thirty-eight, according to Horace Walpole 'because he would not be obliged of those invaluable blessings of an English subject, brandy, small-beer and tobacco'. His only son, another John, was created Baron Spencer of Althorp and Viscount Spencer by George III in 1761, and four years later became the 1st Earl. But before that, when he was plain Mr Spencer, he had married Georgiana Poyntz, a diplomat's daughter, in a secret ceremony at Althorp when the house was full of guests. The day following his twenty-first birthday, after tea, the bride, groom and their four fellow-conspirators withdrew from the assembled company one at a time so as not to be noticed, went upstairs to the Oak Room where they were married by his former tutor, and returned without anyone being any the wiser.

It was John's daughter, Georgiana, who grew into the gorgeous 'Duchess of Dimples', 'the face without a frown' – despite her compulsion for gambling – and who was mistress of the Prince of Wales. It was also the 1st Earl who built Spencer House in London's Piccadilly, overlooking Green Park, now turned into offices. He was MP for Warwick, High Steward of St Albans, and also a patron of the arts – his friends included Sir Joshua Reynolds, who painted his wife with their daughter Georgiana as a little girl, David Garrick the actor, and Charles James Fox, the leading Whig, who became Georgiana's lover when she had grown into a slightly bigger girl. In the famous Westminster elections of 1784 she exchanged kisses for votes for Fox from butchers and other tradesmen in Covent Garden.

Her brother, George, became the 2nd Earl Spencer and married Lavinia Bingham, the beautiful daughter of Lord Lucan, distant relative of the notorious present-day Lord Lucan, who disappeared eight years ago after his children's nanny was murdered at their house in London.

Although the family were traditionally Whigs, George became a Tory and a staunch supporter of William Pitt, with whom his fortunes rose and fell. He became Ambassador to Vienna, Lord Privy Seal, First Lord of the Admiralty at the time of the Battle of Trafalgar, and Secretary of State. During his time as First Lord he became friendly with Horatio Nelson, who also apparently appreciated Lady Spencer's beauty. Not only did he write to Lavinia, he once sent her the sword of a Spanish Admiral, Don Tomaso Geraldino, who had commanded a flagship of eighty-four guns.

George Spencer's political career came to an abrupt end in 1806 with the death of Pitt, so he set about putting Althorp in order. Henry Holland had filled in the moat and begun work on the house some years earlier, while Capability Brown's chief assistant, Samuel Lapidge, had been brought in to help improve the park and gardens. George spent time investigating new farming methods being practised round and about so that he might improve the estate too, and consulted people like his friend the great Coke of Holkham.

George was also Master of Trinity House and an avid collector of books. He was responsible for the famous library at Althorp, said to have been the best in Europe, with its collection of forty thousand early printed books, including fifty-eight Caxtons. It was sold in 1892 for over £200,000, and is now a part of the John Rylands Library at Manchester University.

As if he hadn't contributed enough in his life, George Spencer also invented a new style – a double-breasted tailless waistcoat known as a Spencer. His friend Lord Sandwich invented the sandwich at much the same time, which prompted a contemporary wit to verse:

> Two noble earls, whom, if I quote,
> Some folks might call me sinner,
> The one invented half a coat,
> The other, half a dinner.
> The plan was good, as some will say,
> And fitted to console one,
> Because in this poor starving day,
> Few can afford a whole one.

George and Lavinia had eight children, two of whom died in infancy. The eldest surviving boy, John, born in 1782, was packed off to Harrow at the age of eight, where he met Lord Byron. But he was a shy and awkward boy, and didn't grow up to share his father's rarefied intellectual tastes. Like many of his contemporaries in Regency England he was passionate about sport; he hunted with the Pytchley and never missed the chance of a prize-fight. His second interest was farming, yet, despite an apparent lack of enthusiasm for politics, he was elected MP for Northamptonshire in 1806 and held the seat for thirty years.

John Spencer was a big man, always rather inarticulate, known in the neighbourhood as 'honest Jack Althorp', and was always happier out in the company of dogs and horses than in Society drawing rooms. He would probably never have married had not one Miss Esther Acklom taken a fancy to him. He married her at the age of thirty-two, and they were by all accounts blissfully happy until she died giving birth to a stillborn child. He was devastated and never recovered from her death. He spent the rest of his life dressed in mourning, and devoted himself to politics. When he died twenty-seven years later, he was wearing a locket containing her hair. He became a successful Leader of the House of Commons, Chancellor of the Exchequer under two great Liberals, Grey and Melbourne, and promoter of the First Reform Bill. In 1834 he inherited the title and was able to retire gracefully from the House and go back to farming. As a result of his love of farming, he founded the Royal Agricultural Society of England, and helped to establish the Royal Agricultural College at Cirencester, where Johnnie Althorp was to spend a year studying immediately after his marriage in 1954.

Since 'Honest Jack's' only child had been stillborn, he was succeeded by his brother, Frederick, a naval officer who added a lot of porcelain to the existing collection at Althorp. He had joined the navy when he was thirteen, serving as a midshipman during the Napoleonic Wars when his father, the 2nd Earl, was First Lord of the Admiralty.

Frederick was a Whig MP for ten years after his adventures at sea, then became equerry to the Duchess of Kent – the mother of Queen Victoria – a Privy Councillor, Lord Chamberlain, Rear Admiral and Vice Admiral and finally

Lord Steward of the Household, and was made a Knight of the Garter in 1849. But he was a stern disciplinarian, and not above locking his daughter Sarah in a cupboard under the stairs if she dared to be disobedient.

Frederick was married twice, and it was his son John Poyntz, by his first wife Elizabeth Poyntz – who was also his second cousin – who succeeded him as the 5th Earl in 1857. Always known as the 'Red Earl' because of the colour of his beard, John was passionate about fox-hunting, served three times as Master of the Pytchley Hunt, and often rode out with Empress Elizabeth of Austria, who was a frequent guest at Althorp. He was briefly a Liberal MP for South Northamptonshire in the year before he succeeded to the title. He then became Groom of the Stole to the Prince Consort for two years and to the Prince of Wales, who later became Edward VII, for four. He was Viceroy of Ireland on two occasions, Lord Lieutenant of Northamptonshire, Lord President of the Council, First Lord of the Admiralty, Privy Seal to the Prince of Wales and a member of the Council of the Duchy of Cornwall. The Spencers were becoming indispensable.

In Spencer tradition, the Red Earl married a beautiful woman called Charlotte Seymour, nicknamed 'Spenser's Faerie Queene' because of her looks, but they had no children and so when he died in 1910 the title passed to his half-brother, Charles, Frederick's son by his second wife. The 6th Earl was also an MP, Lord Lieutenant of Northamptonshire, Vice Chamberlain and Lord Chamberlain. And, like the 2nd, 4th and 5th Earls, he was also a Knight of the Garter.

Charles had three daughters and three sons, and the second son was awarded the Croix de Guerre for distinguished service during World War I, and was later killed in a riding accident. The first son, Albert Edward John, known as Jack, was to be Diana's grandfather. He was a godson of Edward VII, and became the 7th Earl in 1922. He had been wounded during the war as a Captain in the First Life Guards, and afterwards devoted himself to Althorp.

In 1919 he, too, had married yet another beautiful woman, Lady Cynthia Hamilton, who was something of a catch, even for a Spencer. She was the 3rd Duke of Abercorn's daughter, and had been ardently wooed during the war by Edward, the Prince of Wales. The Prince, after several love affairs that came to nothing, insisted upon marrying the American divorcee Wallis Simpson, and abdicated the throne to become the Duke of Windsor. In those days it was considered imperative that the heir to the throne should marry someone of royal blood. Had the monarchy been as relaxed then as it is in the 1980s, Lady Cynthia might well have married Edward and the entire course of history would have been very different.

Instead of becoming, albeit posthumously, grandmother of a future queen, Lady Cynthia might have been a queen herself. Sadly she died of cancer in 1972 when Diana was still at preparatory school and, if she had cherished secret hopes of a royal marriage for her granddaughter, it would surely have been with Prince Andrew and not the Prince of Wales.

But Cynthia didn't marry a prince. She married Jack Althorp, a slightly-built, cultured man, who took his inheritance of Althorp seriously and dedicated his life to the house and its treasures. He was a trustee of the Wallace Collection, and loved all works of art, but his own particular hobby was tapestry, and some of the chairs at Althorp are backed with his own work.

Jack was a crusty man, by all accounts, with a short temper. He didn't like people much, and didn't make an effort to hide the fait. He seldom entertained at Althorp, and many of the state rooms were shut up and unused, although in his capacity as Lord Lieutenant of Northamptonshire he was obliged to open up the house for official entertaining from time to time.

He showed off his treasures on his own terms. In the *Daily Telegraph*, journalist Alice Hope recalled being taken round the house on one occasion, but only after the Earl had given her shoes a careful inspection to make sure they were clean enough to walk on his carpets. It wasn't a courtesy he extended to everyone. Other people remember being greeted at the door and treated to his party tricks. He would shake hands with his thumb tucked inside his palm, and say 'Excuse the wart' as the unsuspecting stranger clasped the lump.

It was a rare display of humour. For the most part he was

bad tempered and in every way quite the opposite to his wife. Countess Spencer was 'a real lady': a warm, serene woman whom the locals around Althorp adored. Their loyalty to the Spencers at that time was almost entirely due to their love for her. She mixed with them, and when she came into the villages on the estate, she would always talk to people in a natural, friendly way. People who knew her say Diana has inherited a lot of her qualities.

Though Jack confined himself almost entirely to Althorp, Cynthia continued the Spencer tradition of service to the Crown. She had known the Queen Mother for many years, from the days when she was plain Lady Elizabeth Bowes-Lyon, and their friendship had continued after both their marriages. One year, when Elizabeth was Duchess of York, she and her husband, Bertie, the future George VI, with her two young daughters, Elizabeth and Margaret, had taken a house at Naseby in Northamptonshire to be close to the Spencers for the hunting season. Soon after Bertie became King, in December 1936, Cynthia was appointed first a Lady of the Bedchamber to the Queen, and then a Lady in Waiting, continuing in royal service until her death.

The ties between the two families were close. In addition to Lady Cynthia, Jack's sisters were in service to the Queen Mother too. Lavinia, Lady Annaly, was an Extra Lady in Waiting when Elizabeth was still the Duchess of York; and Lady Delia Peel was Extra Woman of the Bedchamber until 1950.

It is certainly Diana's heritage through her father's line that made her so eligible, genealogically speaking, to marry the Prince of Wales. Her mother's ancestors were far less noble – some of them positively murky – but they do add a little colour to the picture, as well as some Scottish, Irish and even American blood. If the latest expert in such matters is to be believed, she is even descended from the sister of Owen Glendower, the last independent Prince of Wales, so she has some Welsh blood too. What could be more perfect?

The only royal connection in Diana's maternal line came this century when her grandfather, Maurice, the 4th Baron Fermoy, became friends with George V's second son Bertie, then Duke of York. They played tennis together, their wives shared a love of music, and the friendships were further cemented when the King leased to the Fermoys a house on the Sandringham estate, and they thus became neighbours.

The Fermoys originated in Ireland, where Edmund Burke Roche, Diana's great-great-grandfather, was MP for Cork from 1837 to 1855. The following year he was created Baron Fermoy, and towards the end of his life he was Lord Lieutenant of County Cork. Edmund had two sons, and was succeeded by both of them; first, Edward, who died at the age of seventy with no children; and then James, who inherited the title and became the 3rd Baron at the age of sixty-eight.

Here we have to cross the Atlantic briefly, to find his wife, Frances Work, whose mother had been born out of wedlock in India. Her father was rather more respectable, an eccentric millionaire called Frank Work who had begun life as a dry goods clerk from Chillicothe, Ohio, and made his fortune in Manhattan as a stockbroker with the Vanderbilts. Frank Work strongly disapproved of American money marrying into European aristocracy. He believed 'international marriage should be a hanging offence', and threatened to disinherit any of his children who did so. His daughter Frances, known as Fanny, promptly went over to England and married James Boothby Burke Roche, the future 3rd Baron Fermoy, who had impeccable Irish blood but no money.

Eleven years later Fanny returned to New York with her three children (two of them twins) from the marriage, to beg forgiveness from her father. He relented, but decreed that if she and her children were to inherit his fortune, they must promise never to return to Europe to live, or to marry Europeans.

They managed to desist while he was alive, but Fanny obviously found Europeans irresistible, because she did marry another, a Romanian called Auriel Botanyi. Her sons were no better. Soon after her father's death in 1911 both twins, Maurice and Francis, hopped aboard the *Lusitania* to visit Europe, and to 'take in the Coronation of King George V'.

Both boys had been left £600,000 in Frank's will, but to get a penny of it they had to become American citizens within a year of his death and undertake never to visit England again. Although the twins never quite got the full amount, an American court later managed to quash the conditions. Maurice smartly returned to England in 1921 to claim the Fermoy title, as his father, James, whom he had barely known, had died two months after inheriting it himself the previous year.

So Maurice came to England at the age of thirty-five as the 4th Baron Fermoy, and went into politics. As an Irish peer, he was able to stand as a Member of Parliament, so he settled himself at Dersingham in Norfolk, and in 1924 was elected Conservative MP for King's Lynn. He held the seat until 1935, and again for two years during World War II; and in 1931 he was also Mayor of King's Lynn.

That year, at the age of forty-six, he married Ruth Silvia Gill, a twenty-year-old Aberdeenshire girl he had met in Paris, where she was studying the piano under Albert Cortot at the Conservatoire. Their meeting brought her career as a concert pianist to a sudden end and robbed the world of an exceptionally gifted player. It could be argued that King's Lynn got an annual Festival of Music and the Arts as a result – but not until some time later.

After their wedding near her home in Bieldside, Aberdeenshire, the couple moved about from house to house in Norfolk, until George V offered them Park House on the Sandringham estate, which was a good size for their expanding family, and Frances, Diana's mother, was born there in 1936. She was the Fermoys' second child. The first, Mary, was two years older, and a son and heir, Edmund, was born in March 1939. Frances was born the day that George V died, and it is said that the news of her arrival was rushed across the park to Sandringham House where he lay gravely ill and Queen Mary told him of her birth before he died that evening.

The friendship between the Yorks and the Fermoys continued after Bertie's accession as George VI. During World War II the King and Maurice used to play ice-hockey together against visiting American and Canadian troops on the frozen lakes at Sandringham, and in the summer continued to play tennis. Lord Fermoy was out hare shooting with the King

D.-B

19

the day before the latter's death in February 1952. After Maurice Fermoy's own death three years later, his widow Ruth became a Lady in Waiting to her friend Queen Elizabeth, by this time the Queen Mother, and she has remained in her service ever since.

Edmund inherited the title from his father when he was sixteen and still at Eton. Mary and Frances had both married during the previous year: Mary to Viscount Kemsley's son, Anthony Berry, and Frances to Earl Spencer's son, Johnnie, Viscount Althorp. And it was the Althorps who became the next tenants of Park House, thereby escaping from an uneasy proximity to the disagreeable old Earl at Althorp.

Viscount Althorp was born in 1924, four years after his only sister Anne, who was to marry Captain Christopher Wake-Walker in 1944. Johnnie was educated at Eton and Sandhurst, and joined the Scots Greys as soon as he was old enough to fight. He was sent off to the campaign in north-west Europe and was mentioned in dispatches. After World War II he spent three years as ADC to Sir Willoughby Norrie, the Governor of South Australia, and in 1950 became an equerry to George VI – Maurice Fermoy's friend. When the King died, he continued as equerry to the Queen until 1954, when he gave up the job to marry Frances Roche.

Johnnie Althorp was quite a catch for Frances Roche. They had met at the coming-out ball that she shared with her sister at Londonderry House in Park Lane in April 1953, where the Queen Mother had been one of the four hundred guests. She had been brought up at Park House, educated first by a governess and then at Downham School near Bishop's Stortford in Hertfordshire, and before her marriage had spent a few months in Paris and Italy studying art and languages.

When they met, Johnnie was supposedly engaged to Lady Anne Coke of Holkham Hall, eldest daughter of the Earl and Countess of Leicester, and a descendant of the revolutionary farmer, Coke of Holkham, who had helped his ancestor, the 2nd Earl. There was quite a sharp intake of breath in aristocratic drawing rooms around the country when Johnnie ditched Lady Anne in favour of Frances. Frances was only eighteen, while he was thirty-two.

The Queen is said to have attempted to settle things by taking Johnnie away for six months to act for the Master of the Household on the royal tour of Australia; but absence only made the hearts grow fonder. They wrote to each other every day, and when the royal party reached Tobruk he was given permission to go home and prepare for the wedding.

Their wedding was held in Westminster Abbey – Frances was the youngest bride to have been married there this century – and the Queen, the Queen Mother, Prince Philip and Princess Margaret headed a glittering guest list of fifteen hundred people.

Frances, given away by her father, was dressed in a fabulous gown of camellia-white faille embroidered with diamanté, sequins and rhinestones, designed by Eva Lutyens. Her bridesmaids wore replica dresses made of white hailstone muslin, and the pages were dressed in white satin suits with blue sashes, copied from Sir Joshua Reynolds' portrait of *Little Lord Althorp* in his party suit, which hangs in the Marlborough Room at Althorp.

As they left the Abbey, the Royal Scots Greys raised swords for the bride and groom to pass under, and they were swept away to a grand reception at St James's Palace.

'You are making an addition to the home life of your country,' the Bishop of Norwich declared, 'on which above all others, our national life depends.'

How prophetic he turned out to be.

PARK HOUSE

AFTER THE Society wedding of the year, Johnnie and Frances did not begin married life in the kind of prestigious surroundings that either of them had come from, but in a rented house at Rodmarton, while Johnnie studied at the Royal Agricultural College in Cirencester nearby. But, like Charles and Diana, the newly-wed Althorps lost no time in starting a family. Frances became pregnant immediately and in March 1955, just nine months after their wedding, Sarah was born at the Barratt Maternity Home in Northampton. She was christened three months later in St Faith's Chapel in Westminster Abbey, with the Queen Mother as one of her godparents.

By this time the family was living in Orchard Manor, a house on the Althorp estate at Little Creaton. But this was never an ideal situation, for Johnnie and his father didn't see eye to eye. The son had neither his father's intellect nor his erudition. He preferred farming and outdoor activities, and was altogether a far more easy-going character. The Earl was a huntsman who encouraged the fox population, while Johnnie, who had never been interested in horses, preferred shooting. As anyone who has tried to rear pheasant chicks knows, foxes and chicks just don't mix.

Johnnie's marriage to Frances didn't help. The old Earl needed diplomatic treatment, and Frances was never prepared to kow-tow to him. She tolerated his bad manners as barely as he tolerated her spirit, and as a result the relationship between father and son grew worse.

So it came as a great relief to everyone when, after the death of Lord Fermoy later that year, her mother suggested to Frances that she and Johnnie should take over Park House on the Sandringham estate. It was a large family house, with ten bedrooms in all, and extended servants' quarters and garages, built in the nineteenth century by Edward VII, then Prince of Wales, who had bought the estate near the west coast of Norfolk in 1861.

Park House lay down a sweeping gravel drive, with neat lawns on either side, and wonderful old trees and shrubs. These screened the house from the road on one side, while on the other it looked out over Sandringham cricket pitch and acres of parkland. The house was built of brick faced with the local carrstone, which gave it a rough texture and, because of its dark colour, a rather bleak appearance. Inside it was far from bleak: it was a warm, comfortable family home, where Diana was to be born in 1961.

In fact the house had not originally been intended as a family home: like several others in the grounds, it had been built by the Prince of Wales to accommodate his staff and hordes of friends he liked to have with him at Sandringham. York Cottage, where George VI and Queen Elizabeth used to stay when they were Duke and Duchess of York, was another of these, now serving as the estate office and flats.

West Norfolk wasn't Johnnie's patch at all, and his first job after the move to Park House was to find something to do with himself. In time he would inherit Althorp and have fifteen thousand acres to manage, but for the present he needed land closer to home. He soon found himself a small 250-acre farm at Ingoldisthorpe, a few miles from Sandringham, which he bought for £16,000. Fourteen months later Frances spent £20,000 on a further 236 acres at Snettisham for him and later on bought more land at Heacham, all of which adjoined the original farm and brought the total to roughly 650 acres, on which he farmed beef cattle.

Not long after they had settled in, their second daughter, Jane, was born in 1957 in the Queen Elizabeth Maternity Home in King's Lynn, six weeks prematurely. This time, the Duke of Kent becme a godfather. Two years later Frances was pregnant again, and on 12 January 1960 she had a boy, delivered in her bedroom at Park House. They called him John, but he only survived for ten hours. His grave now lies

23

alongside his grandfather's, Maurice Fermoy, in the west corner of the churchyard at Sandringham. The grave to the other side of baby John Spencer's marks another family tragedy. It belongs to Elizabeth Roche, Edmund Fermoy's daughter, who survived for only six days after her birth in March 1966.

Frances Althorp must have felt, in the inevitable depression that followed her baby's death, that she was nothing better than a producer of sons to the aristocracy. She had matured since her marriage at eighteen. The Johnnie who had then swept her off her feet, who had appeared the embodiment of the exciting, sophisticated and worldly older man, had now settled comfortably into married monotony and middle age. Her life must have suddenly seemed very dull and empty.

More important, behind closed doors Johnnie is said to have displayed another side to his character – not the mild, kindly side the locals knew. To them he was the perfect gent. Ray Hunt, the electrician who installed a television set in Frances's bedroom the day after Diana was born, spoke for them all when he said, 'Earl Spencer is as nice a man as you could ever wish to meet'. As a husband, however, it was a different matter, but Frances continued to live with Johnnie and persevere for the boy he wanted so badly.

She became pregnant again later that year, and on Saturday, 1 July 1961 Diana was born at Park House. Her weight was 7lb 12oz, and she was hailed by her father as 'a perfect physical specimen'. But her names were not yet recorded; her parents had so wanted a son that they hadn't considered girls' names.

Early the following week the local registrar, John Wilson, called in at Park House to register the birth and sign the birth certificate. By this time Frances and Johnnie had settled on the names: Diana Frances.

So Diana Frances was despatched to the nursery, to her cream-papered room overlooking the drive, and to a new nanny called Judith, a girl from Kent who had joined the household just three months earlier. Diana was christened on 30 August amid the splendours of Sandringham Church, officially St Mary Magdalene, by the rector, the Right Reverend Percy Herbert. St Mary's is an unforgettable church, with a dramatic solid silver altar, and brilliantly rich colours in the windows, walls and vaults. The bapistry is at the base of the tower, and Diana was christened, surrounded by gilded angels and the colours of the Royal Norfolk Regiment, in a Florentine marble font that had been given by Edward VII.

That was the nearest she came to royalty at her christening. Ironically, Diana was the only one of the Spencer children not to have a royal godparent. Her godfathers were John Floyd, now Chairman of Christie's, the auctioneers, who had been at Eton and Sandhurst with her father, and Johnnie's first cousin, Alexander Gilmour, now a director of Carr Sebag & Co., and half-brother of Sir Ian Gilmour, the former Conservative Lord Privy Seal. Her godmothers were Lady Mary Colman, wife of the Lord Lieutenant of Norfolk, a relative of the Queen Mother and formerly an Extra Lady in Waiting to Princess Alexandra; Sarah Pratt, who lived nearby at Ryston Hall, Downham Market; and Carol Fox, another near neighbour who lived at Anmer Hall, now the home of the Duke and Duchess of Kent. Diana's godparents weren't royal, but they weren't nobodies.

When Diana's mother had spent her childhood at Park House, it was run with a full complement of staff as befitted their status and the period. But by the time Diana was born in 1961, Johnnie and Frances had no need for such grandeur. The only entertaining they would have to do would be purely social. There was far less formality about the place, but it was still by most people's standards a formal household. The staff, albeit reduced in number, had their territory marked out. The cook would scarcely have known her way to the nursery, let alone have ever in her wildest dreams thought of bathing the baby; not even in an emergency. The nanny, likewise, would have known better than to try to boil herself an egg. And neither cook nor nanny went uninvited beyond the swing doors that divided staff from family.

The Spencer children, as and when they arrived, lived in the nursery wing, and were brought up along very traditional lines. They were taught to eat what they were given, never to interrupt, never to speak with their mouths full, to sit up straight at table, to smile and be polite to people, to shake hands when being introduced to someone, to play quietly and talk nicely, and to keep the nursery neat and tidy.

The nursery wing consisted of three bedrooms, a bathroom and one large nursery, and was all on the first floor, set off at a tangent to the main body of the house, above the butler's pantry and other domestic rooms.

Diana had a lot of attention as a baby. Sarah and Jane, respectively aged six and four when Diana was born, were at school during the mornings, even if it was only downstairs, where they were taught by the governess. So, for a large part of the day, Diana had the nursery to herself; and when her sisters were there they treated her as their own personal property, helping to bath her, dress her and to brush her hair.

After lunch, which was always good nursery fare, the children went out for a walk, with Diana in a large old-fashioned pram. Sometimes Judith would take them for their walk; at other times it would be Frances. Locals remember seeing them out walking, and say how friendly Lady Althorp was, how she would always stop for a chat, and how bubbly and pretty the little girls were.

The countryside around Park House is an irresistible invitation to even the most reluctant walker. When Edward VII bought Sandringham in 1861 the estate consisted of eight thousand acres, but today it spreads over twenty thousand; some farmland, some woodland with wide pathways running through and with rides and a carpet of heather.

But locals pick their time to take walks, and in the open pheasant season, they drive. Sandringham is one of the greatest shooting estates in the country, and not one which the Royal Family could ever be accused of neglecting. Lord Althorp used to shoot on the estate in his time there too. The one room that the children were forbidden to go into at Park House was the gun room. Johnnie took his shooting very seriously, keeping gun dogs that lived out of doors in kennels by the garages, and were let into the house on pain of death.

The Royal Family wasn't the Spencers' nearest neighbour, and of course wasn't at Sandringham for much of the year anyway. So the two families were never so friendly that they were forever in one another's houses. But if the Queen was out riding in the park, for instance, and spotted one of the Spencer children in their garden, she would always come over and talk to them for a moment. And the children would go to tea with each other, particularly the younger ones who were closer in age. In later years when Johnnie had built a heated swimming pool at Park House, Prince Andrew, Prince Edward and Princess Margaret's children frequently came over to swim.

Their closest neighbours – not more than a stone's throw away – were, in fact, the Reverend Patrick Ashton and his family, who moved into the rectory when Diana was small. Across the park was Laycocks where the Loyds lived. Julian Loyd was, and still is, land agent at Sandringham, and his two children, Alexandra and Charles, were much the same age as Diana and her younger brother Charles. So the children with whom Diana played far more frequently than she ever played with the royals were Penelope Ashton, the rector's daughter, and Alexandra Loyd.

Diana made her first public appearance in front of the cameras at the age of twenty months, although only in a supporting role in those days. This took place in March 1963 at a civic reception for her grandmother, Ruth, Lady Fermoy, in honour of her being made a Freeman of the Borough of King's Lynn, for her 'work in music and art in West Norfolk'.

Ruth had always been a great music lover and was a profound influence on Diana's own musical taste. When she had come to King's Lynn in 1931, the year that she married Lord Fermoy, the former music student found her new home town a musical waste land. So, after the war, she began to organize and sometimes to play lunchtime concerts. In March 1950 she played a Schumann piano concerto at the Royal Albert Hall for the Queen Mother. The next year she launched the King's Lynn Festival to celebrate the opening of the restored St George's Guildhall, now known as the Fermoy Centre. For the next twenty-five years, the Queen Mother was the Festival's patron, with Ruth as chairman.

In May 1964, when Diana was almost three, her little brother Charles was born, away from home at the London Clinic, but the news was phoned through straightaway and everyone in the house was jubilant. The entire household had been waiting with bated breath, terrified that the new baby would prove to be another girl. But no, at last a boy, an heir and a healthy one. The flags flew that day at Althorp: bells would have rung too at St Mary's, the local church, but the tower was not deemed safe enough.

Charles was christened in great style in Westminster Abbey soon after Diana's third birthday. The Queen was one of his godmothers and the whole family was there with one exception – the birthday girl. Diana had fallen down a flight of stone steps the day before and was nursing a large bruise on her head.

Her disappointment was quickly forgotten when she heard that instead she would be going to her Uncle Edmund's wedding in London. This was Frances's younger brother, the 5th Lord Fermoy, who was married to Lavinia Pitman at the Guards' Chapel at Wellington Barracks. And once again Diana was a scene-stealer, dressed up in her new smart coat and straw hat.

Now that she was no longer the baby of the family, Diana had to knuckle down to a morning's work with the family's governess, Ally – not that it was so very strenuous at first. All the children worked at their own pace – they did, after all, span a wide age group. And Diana, at the age of four, was rather more interested in painting, cutting-out and sticking than investigating the kings and queens of England, or rattling off her twelve times table like her elder sisters. In fact, she may have listened to more than anyone realized while she sloshed away with her glue. Ally used to say that she showed particular interest in history in those first few years, and at West Heath she was always to be fascinated by the Tudors and Stuarts.

When school was over Diana and her sisters might go off shopping in the car with their mother, sometimes into Snettisham, the best-stocked of the villages nearby, and sometimes into King's Lynn, which involved more of an expedition. Or they might go up to their father's farm to see the new calves that had been born. And in the summer, if they could nag enough, they would go off to the seaside at Brancaster, about twenty minutes' drive away on the north coast of Norfolk, where the family had a beach hut. At the weekends they might even take a picnic lunch with them and go for the whole day.

But they very rarely went across to Althorp, and only their mother would take them. Johnnie would never go; and his father never came to Park House. The Countess Spencer came to stay from time to time, particularly when the Queen Mother was at York Cottage. Cynthia used to come to watch Johnnie play at the annual cricket match each summer, a great occasion celebrated with much jollification. Johnnie played for the President's XI, which was run by Julian Loyd, and every year they took on the local cricket club.

The children all had bicycles and Sarah and Jane had a pony called Romany, which they kept tethered out in the park. He wasn't the friendliest beast and was not averse to biting the hand that offered him a sugar lump.

Each year the children's birthdays were celebrated with parties to which all their friends came, while the Spencer fireworks party on 5 November was a great event in the social calendar. A crowd of children used to come wrapped up in their scarves and woolly hats, and warm up with hot sausages while Johnnie acted as Master of Ceremonies and set off a great arsenal of rockets and Catherine wheels, bangers, squibs and whizzers.

But in September 1967 this intimate and happy family group began to disband and life gradually changed at Park House. This started with Sarah and Jane going off to boarding school at West Heath in Kent, away from home for the first time. Since neither had ever been away to day school, the house was very strange without them.

Then, in autumn 1967, Frances departed, and she and Johnnie began a trial separation. Diana was six, and Charles was three and a half. Even now, fourteen years later, the leaving and the divorce that followed are subjects that Frances will never talk about, not even to her closest friends.

Her reasons for leaving were not as selfish as people have been led to assume. For a long time she has been cast as the villainess, and her husband as the wronged man. But no one has explained why, if that was true, all four of those children that she 'deserted' should be so fond of her.

She left because she had been unhappy with Johnnie for years. Sweet and kind and gentle as a father though he was, he was quite another man as a husband; just as his own father had been with his wife. Cynthia had put up with it, but Frances was of a tougher mettle, and she had now found someone else with whom she believed she could be happy. She had fallen in love with Peter Shand Kydd, a wealthy man who, at the time they first met, had been happily married with three children. He was entirely different from Johnnie, and, apart from the sheer thrill of the affair, she had no doubt found the contrast enormously exciting. He was bohemian where Johnnie had been straitlaced, and witty and fun where Johnnie had been staid and dull.

Frances also believed that it would be better for the children to see their parents apart but happy, rather than to cope with them living under the same roof and fighting with each other the whole time. She felt that if she were happy she could be a better mother to them. No doubt there were difficult scenes in the privacy of their own home. In public, however, appearances were kept up until the day she was gone.

And so she left them, but not mysteriously. She told all the children that she was leaving and why: she went to great trouble to explain it, although she feared that only the older two had understood.

Many find it hard to understand how a mother could leave four children, including one just three years old, but Frances would have had no idea when she did leave them behind that she would be doing so permanently. Even in those days it was practically unheard of for custody of the children from a marriage to be given to their father. The mother would have had to have a fairly wicked picture painted of her by those contesting the case for a court to take her children away from her, particularly the young ones.

Frances therefore would have left in every expectation that it would be a temporary arrangement. In fact, initially the two younger children were with her. The day after Frances left, Johnnie put Diana and Charles on a train with their nanny and all three stayed with her in London until Christmas. Frances took the children back to Park House for Christmas, but it became obvious that there was no chance of saving the marriage, so the children stayed in Norfolk. Frances believed that she was doing the best thing: she knew they adored their father and that they would be perfectly well looked after. Life at Park House would go on without much more than a hiccup.

Her departure, however, was not really the tremendous surprise that people have suggested. Most of the staff at Park House had seen it coming, and they by no means condemned her. Mrs Violet Collison, who had been a housemaid, even went with her as a cook. Another departure at Christmas, possibly more important from the children's point of view, was that of their nanny, a local girl who had looked after Charles and Diana for two years. She had become almost as much a part of their lives as their mother.

The person who was probably most surprised and shocked of all was Johnnie. He loved Frances, and had never thought in his wildest dreams that she would leave him. When she did, he was devastated.

But condemnation came from an unexpected quarter: her own family. Her mother, Ruth, Lady Fermoy, was appalled by what her daughter had done, with the result that she and Frances didn't speak to one another for years.

A number of her acquaintances in Norfolk turned against her too, and gossip was unleashed anew in April 1968 when Frances was branded as 'the other woman' in the Shand Kydds' divorce. Peter didn't contest the case: he lost custody of his three children and was ordered to pay costs.

Nowadays people in West Norfolk simply say Frances was young and must have given in to temptation: she was a strikingly pretty woman, full of life, vivacious and fun to be with – but she was always strong-willed and determined. Johnnie, they say, was a wonderful sweet kind man, a model father, but no one ever says he was a man with much spark or get-up-and-go.

In December 1968 Frances began divorce proceedings against Johnnie on the grounds of his cruelty. If she had won the case she would in all probability have been given custody of the children. But Johnnie contested it; and he could call to his

31

aid as witnesses on his behalf some of the highest names in the land. In the circumstances, Frances didn't stand a chance, and the case was dismissed.

Four months later Johnnie was granted a divorce from Frances on the grounds of her adultery with Peter Shand Kydd 'at an address', it was clinically pinpointed, 'in South Kensington in April or May 1967'. Since Peter Shand Kydd had not contested his divorce, there was no way Frances could now contest Johnnie's accusation. The case went through undefended, and the price she had to pay was custody of her children. Frances was officially granted access to the children, but both before and after the proceedings Johnnie had allowed her to see them and to have them for the weekend in London. He may have been hurt by what happened, but he never tried to use his children as weapons against her.

Frances and Peter Shand Kydd, neither of them the toast of London, married that same year in a very quiet register office wedding, and went to live on the coast in West Sussex.

Frances had first met Peter Shand Kydd at a dinner party in London. She was there with Johnnie, while Peter was accompanied by his wife, a lovely, talented artist called Janet Munro Kerr. Both couples ostensibly got on well and not long afterwards went off on a skiing holiday together with one other couple. On their return to London Peter, who was then forty-two and had been married for sixteen years, moved out of his home and left his wife and their three children. At first his wife was philosophical about it, and rather than insisting he give up this other woman or else, thought it wisest to let him go off in the belief that he would get it out of his system and come back to her. But Peter Shand Kydd was easily led, and Frances more than happy to do the leading. Janet now realises that had she handled the situation differently her marriage might have been saved.

The Shand Kydds had recently come back to England after three years farming in Australia. Peter had inherited the family wallpaper business after the war – his elder brother was killed in an aeroplane crash – but he was never a particularly dedicated businessman. He was a bit of a gypsy, as someone described him; never happy in one place for long, dabbling in different ventures. He had been educated at Marlborough

College and Edinburgh University, and had spent the war in the navy, joining up on the very day that he was old enough. He had fallen in love with Australia on a business trip there, and so in August 1963 Peter resigned from the board of Shand Kydd, although he kept his shares in the company, and he and Janet and the three children emigrated to farm a five-hundred-acre sheep station he had bought near Young in New South Wales. He then bought more land near Yass, about nineteen miles away; but the venture was not altogether successful, and after three years he cut his losses, sold the original farm, and the family came back to England. By this time the family firm had merged with and were finally taken over by Reed Decorative Products, a subdivision of Reed International. Peter began to dabble in other things; he even started a pottery.

Peter Shand Kydd has since gone back to farming and it is now his main livelihood. He has kept the additional patch of land that he bought in Australia, and in 1972 Frances bought an adjoining farm. They now have a total of a thousand acres, which they go out to twice a year although, curiously, Diana had never been to Australia with them until February 1981, just before her engagement was announced.

The rest of the year they spend on a hill farm in the west of Scotland, on the Isle of Seil, which they also bought in 1972. Peter farms sheep and cattle, and Frances breeds pint-sized Shetland ponies, which she shows all over Scotland. She also owns a gift shop in Oban, and spends a lot of her time behind the counter. They have another farm near Perth in Scotland, and still maintain a flat in London in Warwick Square, where they stay on their trips south.

Throughout all this domestic turmoil, Diana remained a courageous little girl. She carried on with her life as though nothing had happened. Her friends had all been told by their parents that Diana's mother had gone, but at six none of them really had any idea of what this meant. They noticed that Diana might snap at them occasionally, which was uncharacteristic, and occasionally they found her crying, but not often. All around the grown-ups in her life made an effort to keep her occupied.

Both grandmothers came to the rescue in the winter of 1967.

It wasn't only the children who needed help; Johnnie was in a bad way too, and their support was a great relief to him. Neither grandmother was particularly practical when it came to dealing with the children, but Sarah and Jane coped with the little ones during the Christmas holidays, and they all got by. With everyone there Christmas itself was as exciting as it ever had been, and friends, relations and neighbours saw to it that the family was never without an invitation. Yet, however jolly everyone managed to make Christmas, the house was no longer a happy one, and when Sarah and Jane both packed their trunks and went off to school in January, it became quieter than ever.

But Diana had plenty to take her mind off things. She and Charles had a new nanny called Sally who had to be instructed in the ways of the nursery, and Diana took great pride in being able to show her where everything in her own bedroom belonged, and how many sugars they were allowed in their tea.

She was a punctiliously tidy little girl even then. Her bedroom was immaculate. There was never a sock out of place and her toys were neatly arranged on shelves or in cupboards; and when it came to clearing up the nursery at the end of the day, she never had to be bullied.

Diana never played with any one toy for long. She was on the go all day long, and quite exhausting to be with. This seemed to be her method of dealing with her problems. She refused to allow herself to think or to notice that Mummy wasn't there. She also began to talk far more than anyone ever remembers her talking either before, or later in her life. She chattered constantly from the moment she got up in the morning to the time she went to bed.

The other distraction in her life was school. The family had decided that Diana and Charles would both be better off out of the house and in the happy atmosphere of a school where they would be able to mix with other children. So, early in January 1968, they were both enrolled at a local day school in King's Lynn, where Diana began the schooldays she 'adored'.

THE SCHOOL YEARS

DIANA'S academic career had begun in the school room at
Park House. It was a ground-floor room, in between the
drawing room and the kitchen, where the children could sit at
their desks and gaze out of the large sash windows at
Sandringham park and grazing cattle, and, but for the hawk
eyes of old Ally, might have happily dreamed the day away.

Ally was a white-haired lady in her sixties who came up to
Park House every weekday morning from her cottage in
Dersingham a couple of miles away to teach a select bunch of
local children. Her real name was Miss Gertrude Allen and it
was she who had taught Frances and her brother and sister,
although in those days they had called her Gert. In the
intervening twenty years or so she had reigned over her patch
in West Norfolk, teaching a clique of well-bred young boys and
girls to read and write and preparing them for entrance to all
the major preparatory and public schools in the country.

The very idea of a private governess in the 1960s might
sound remarkable and would have been in any other county in
Great Britain. But life has changed very little in Norfolk over
the years. It is still intensely feudal even now: the land, all
highly fertile, is divided up amongst a handful of wealthy
aristocrats or bankers with big houses and good connections.
They employ the locals to run their houses and their land, and
the locals, loyal to a man, know their place and keep to it.

There are no longer many private governesses; Ally died
just a month before Diana's wedding and virtually took an era
with her. But nannies still look after the children in Norfolk
homes, cooks rule the kitchens, and cleaners polish up the
silver, while the parents work hard and play hard, involving
themselves in good works within the county, raising pheasants

for the season, and organizing jolly good 'dos'. And until the bomb of Frances's departure in the autumn of 1967, the Althorp parents and children fitted comfortably into the pattern.

But Diana never really got much further than the rudiments of learning with Ally, because a few weeks after her mother left home, in November 1967, Ally left too.

Ally's long years of teaching at Park House were at last at an end – and it must have saddened her not to see the younger children through their early years of schooling. When Frances first went to London during her trial separation from Johnnie, Diana and Charles were sent to appropriate schools near their house in South Eaton Place. Instead, Ally turned her experienced attentions to children from other Norfolk families.

After their rather difficult Christmas at Park House, and in the absence of any permanent nanny, Diana and Charles were sent off to begin proper school in a little private day establishment in King's Lynn called Silfield School.

It was Diana's godmother, Carol Fox, who recommended Silfield School. Her two children, William and Annabel, were there, and not only were they pleased with the school, but it also seemed sensible to send Diana to a place where she would already know some of the children. Alexandra Loyd, her friend from across the park, was also starting the same term which made it easier still. It was a small family school which taught the children on much the same lines as Diana had experienced with Ally: old-fashioned discipline and learning by rote. There were only fifteen children to a class; girls and boys mixed, and two age groups mixed in each class so again, as with Ally, they were not all doing the same things. There were also plenty of outdoor activities, netball and rounders and other sorts of team games, which took place on the tennis court and in the garden at the back of the house.

Everything happened at the back of the house. The entire school consisted of a collection of wooden outbuildings in the garden of a large house in Gayton Road. Unless given specific instructions, a passer-by would never have known it was a school. The children only ever came into the house to use the lavatory, to hang up their coats, or for lunch, which they ate off long low yellow-topped tables in the dining room.

Charles was almost four when they began at Silfield School, so he went into the nursery section which took the three- to four-year-olds for the mornings only. Diana went into Class 1, a mixture of five- and six-year-olds; and Jean Lowe, the headmistress, remembers being very pleased with the good grounding that Diana had obviously had at the hands of her governess. She recalls that she was a fluent reader in that first term, and had good clear handwriting.

Miss Lowe was enormously impressed by the way Johnnie dealt with his children: right on time to collect them, careful to put their wellington boots in the right place, and punctilious in going into the classroom to see the work that both children had been doing, and to talk to their friends.

Johnnie took the children to school and collected them as often as he could, but he organized a rota with other parents in the Sandringham area to do the seven-mile school run each day. And when he was away, it would be Ernie Smith, the gardener at Park House – Smithy as Diana called him – who drove them all.

Diana was perhaps quieter than most of the children to begin with, but then she had lived a very cocooned existence up to that point. She had never been amongst strangers, never been into a building on her own that didn't belong to either a friend or a relation, never played team games, and never been exposed to the boisterousness of gangs of little girls and boys, and the teasing and the jokes.

But she adapted very quickly, helped no doubt by having her friends at hand, and by a particularly sensitive father who tried to make up for his wife's absence in every way he could. Everyone around her did their best to compensate, to treat the two children with kid gloves, expecting the cheerful façade to break at any moment. But Diana appeared to have an inner resilience.

Individual competition was discouraged at Silfield School. Miss Lowe was a firm believer that team work was best, and the children were therefore all divided into three houses, Red, Blue and Green, and they all wore badges on their chests to show which house they belonged to. There were for that reason no individual marks for either work or games. Weekly spelling tests and tables tests were held, and if the child did well, his or her marks went towards the house: likewise, out on the netball court, or on sports day.

There is no real knowing whether Diana's work suffered. Miss Lowe says that although she arrived with a good grounding, she was never academically very hopeful. Her brother Charles, on the other hand, was a solemn little boy, but clever right from the start. Diana was never solemn. She was well-mannered, neat and a sensible sort of child, but cheerful, bright and mischievous with the best of them.

One quality that struck her teachers and friends even then was her interest in the younger children. She used to enjoy going into the nursery class and helping the little ones at Silfield and she was always like a mother hen with Charles. It was as though she had taken over her mother's role. She had the same maternal instinct that most little girls have, but where most of them channel it into dolls, Diana's was let loose on the real thing.

School began at 9 o'clock, so there was a scramble each morning to get them both dressed, Diana in her uniform of grey skirt and red jumper and tights, and breakfasted before it was time to leave. Breakfast was one of the two meals in the day that the new nanny prepared herself in the nursery. There was a corner cupboard in the room with cereals in it, and all the cutlery and china they needed.

On dry days the children spent all their free time in the school garden. There was a large sand pit to play in, and swings, and a patch of lawn beyond the tennis court known as Hipkin's Lawn, although hardly anyone ever knew why. It was, in fact, named after the gardener who made it; who had carefully relaid all the turves taken off the old grass tennis court when it was converted years before.

School finished at 3.30 p.m. and it was nearly 4 o'clock by the time Diana arrived home for tea – sandwiches and biscuits in the nursery, and a good supply of freshly made cakes and buns that the cook had sent up. In winter, when it was dark by the time that tea was over, there was always a big log fire in the nursery and television to watch. In summer, they could ride bikes out in the gravel drive and on the tennis court, or play games on the lawn and the cricket pitch, swim in the new pool, or climb the trees in the beech wood at the front. The garden at Park House was a child's paradise. The swimming pool was the only heated one around and quite an attraction for all the local children. They loved watching it being built too: there were great piles of earth to climb on and hundreds of frogs appeared, hopping about in the vast hole in the ground. No expense was spared: there was a diving board and a blue slide, which the children all adored, and a sophisticated underwater light which revolved, flashing different colours by night.

On weekday evenings, after he had been busy all day, Johnnie would come up to the nursery to spend time with the children before they went to bed, and to see any drawings they had brought home from school, although he left the bedtime story to the nanny. Diana's drawings and paintings were always dedicated 'To Mummy and Daddy', and once her teacher at school had expressed concern about this, but no one ever made an incident out of it. And Diana never made any comment. She didn't talk about her mother at all, nor did she mention any of her previous nannies. Diana and Charles did still see their mother, and she was a constant presence about the house, if only in photographs with children in her arms. Johnnie hadn't had a purge. And during the first term at Silfield School they were both packed off on the train from King's Lynn to Liverpool Street, escorted by their nanny, to spend the weekend with their mother in London.

They were thrilled to bits, partly at the thought of seeing their mother, but also because of the sheer delight of going on a train, which made the coming back very much easier. They had to say goodbye, which was sad, but they were going to travel on the train again. So there were no tears; and Frances didn't allow herself to show any emotion either. From then on, both parents did their utmost to make their separation as easy and painless as possible for the children.

Diana would never talk about Frances at Park House; she had clearly understood that her mother didn't live there any more. But she did fret about Johnnie if he was gone for long.

She would always ask, 'When's Daddy coming home?' and was delighted when he did come. But they were never physically demonstrative. Johnnie was kindly and sensitive and patient as a father, but he had a reserve towards his children, which he was unable to overcome, however much he would have liked to. He was a product of his own very formal upbringing. His was the sort of household where fathers shook hands with their sons rather than kissing them, and stood and watched their daughters at play rather than getting down on the floor with them.

Charles would occupy himself for hours with toy trains and cars which he drove endlessly round and round in patterns on the floor. Diana wasn't particularly interested in cars and even less interested in dolls. She had the usual menagerie of furry animals on her bed, but there wasn't any one that she was inseparable from, and her teddy bear spent his days aloof on a shelf in the nursery.

There was one time when he was brought down. One cold, miserable afternoon when Diana had run out of jobs like the washing up and the shoe polishing, with which she always liked to help, Sally, the nanny, discovered a drawer full of baby clothes in the nursery, which presumably had belonged to Charles. Diana was entranced and she spent the rest of the afternoon dressing up her teddy bear in stretch suits and little woolly hats.

A teddy bear might have done for one afternoon, but he wasn't a patch on the real thing, and Diana had the real thing in the form of Charles. She bossed him about in the most maternal fashion – never unkindly, but always quite firmly. She was a confident and very strong-willed young lady in those days and if it was time for Charles to pack away his toys because it was bath time, then she didn't expect to have to put up with any arguments. She was far closer to Charles than to either of her sisters. They were, after all, closer in age, and spent far more time together in the early years. She still adores him, but probably has more in common with Jane nowadays.

The confidence is something that deserted Diana in later years. But at six she was as bright and chatty as all the other children in her class at Silfield School. Children with divorced parents who come into Miss Lowe's care always have a special eye kept on them to make sure they are coping, but Diana was never any problem at all. In her school work she never shone, but no one put that down to having no mother any more. And she always tried. She had always been a great tryer, and nothing could be more evident of that than the way in which she has all but conquered her public shyness in her role as Princess of Wales, with its obvious rewards.

At seven she also reaped the rewards. Johnnie managed to persuade officials at Dudley Zoo to lend him a camel for the afternoon, and Diana had a birthday party which she is never likely to forget.

It was all a tremendous surprise. Diana and her guests expected nothing more exciting than musical bumps and jellies, when suddenly they were all told to stand in a straight line, and a huge camel came ambling across the lawn, with a keeper in tow. A pin could have been heard to drop as twenty-odd awe-struck boys and girls lined up beside the special mounting block that had been erected, and took turns in sitting on the creature's back, two at a time, and being walked up and down the garden.

Johnnie said that he had organized the surprise because Diana had worked so hard at school that term that he wanted to give her and her friends a special birthday treat. And they did get to their jellies in the end: they had tea out on the lawn with a large birthday cake with seven candles.

When she broke up from school at the end of that summer term she went off to spend the first of many summers divided between two homes – her mother's, which was now in Cadogan Place, and the place she always regarded as 'home', Park House.

Frances was by this time married to Peter Shand Kydd, for whom Diana had fallen almost as soundly as her mother. One quality she has always had is a generous acceptance of people who are friendly to her. This was partly where she scored such a huge success with the press in the months leading up to her engagement to Prince Charles. It also explains why, out of all the Spencer children, she was the one who most accepted. Raine, their father's new wife, when she swept into their lives.

The two were complete opposites in every way, but she never made her step-mother feel unwelcome. Confrontation was never her style.

The following year, in 1969, Diana was a bridesmaid for the first time when her cousin Elizabeth Wake-Walker became a Duckworth-Chad at St James's, Piccadilly. By this time Frances and Peter Shand Kydd had bought a house with a big garden at Itchenor on the Sussex coast, and that summer Diana spent her mother's share of her holiday mucking about in boats there, swimming in the sea and, if she could be persuaded to stay out of the water long enough, playing croquet on the lawn, before they got down to the more serious business of getting her kitted out for Riddlesworth Hall, her new school.

Silfield School had served its purpose admirably, and Diana had been happy there, but there were long periods in the evenings and at weekends when she was unoccupied, and when Johnnie couldn't always guarantee to be there. By this time he had taken on many duties and activities, and was certainly no lord of leisure. There were his farms at Snettisham and Ingoldisthorpe to manage, more than six hundred acres in all, as well as the management of Park House itself. He had just been made Honorary Colonel of the Northamptonshire Territorials and was still on the Northamptonshire County Council, all of which took time. And every time he attended a meeting it was a good four hours' drive away. Then there were inevitable functions he had to go to, and public relations exercises. On top of all this he was Chairman of the National Association of Boys' Clubs, which involved travelling all over the country visiting boys' clubs, and locally he was involved in amateur operatics.

Meanwhile, Diana and Charles had a succession of girls and au pairs who, although kind enough, couldn't provide the sort of stability that everyone agreed Diana needed. She was now nine, and it was decided that she might do better both emotionally and academically in a boarding school.

Both her aunt, Lady Wake-Walker, and her godmother, Sarah Pratt, suggested Riddlesworth Hall. Their own daughters, Diana and Claire, were already there and very happy. It seemed ideal: it was a small friendly school with only one hundred and twenty girls, aged between seven and thirteen, just about two hours' drive from Park House, and set in thirty-two acres of Norfolk countryside, where Diana would feel as at home as anywhere. The headmistress was Miss Elizabeth Ridsdale, known as Riddy to the girls, a spinster by circumstance rather than dedication, with all the warmth and humour of someone who feels she has raised not just one family but generations of them.

As it still sets out in the school prospectus: 'The basis of a good education has always been the family, and a boarding school should provide a stable family atmosphere in which a child can develop naturally and happily. Where individual freedom and the discipline of a community are in easy balance, a sense of security can be achieved and every child will have the opportunity to be good at something.'

Before the school term began in September, Frances took Diana to the school outfitter, Harrods in Knightsbridge, to buy her uniform. She needed grey divided skirts, white Aertex shirts, grey knee-length socks and a cherry red twin set for everyday wear; and for Sundays, a pair of heavy black walking shoes for going to church, gloves, a grey Harris tweed coat and a grey hat with a cherry headband. In summer she had to wear a turquoise-coloured fine wool dress, which tickled like crazy, and a panama hat. There was games equipment to buy too, plimsolls for gym and tennis shoes; and bed linen and towels. Finally everything, but everything, had to be clearly marked with her name.

Riddlesworth Hall was a success. Diana arrived in the autumn of 1970, a quiet, rather introverted little girl, who kept her head down in the way that is still her trademark, and stayed at one remove from everything that was going on around her. She was homesick to begin with, although there is nothing unusual in that; most girls are homesick when they first go away to school.

But she began with one advantage: she arrived at the same time as Alexandra Loyd, while Diana Wake-Walker and Claire Pratt were already in the school, plus one or two other familiar faces from Silfield, so it wasn't as grim as it might have

D.-C

43

been. And it wasn't many weeks before the friendliness, the busyness and the general fun of life at Riddlesworth broke down Diana's reserve and she began to come out of herself. As contemporaries have said, 'You couldn't not be happy at Riddlesworth, it's just like one big happy family.'

Riddlesworth was run along much the same lines as Silfield. The girls were divided into houses, not for sleeping purposes, but for competitive purposes as at Silfield. Good and bad work marks, for instance, went for or against the house, not the individual, and there were inter-house sports. Sometimes they were not so competitive and simply all went off on house picnics and outings. There were three houses, Cavell, Fry and Nightingale, and Diana was in Nightingale.

The teaching methods were also formal and traditional as at Silfield, and good manners and consideration for others were as much a part of life as getting out of bed in the morning. But in every other respect the schools were poles apart. Three functional wooden outhouses in a back garden on the outskirts of the town of King's Lynn were exchanged for a very pretty neoclassical sandstone mansion, set in acres of fertile countryside, while Hipkin's Lawn made way for Big and Little Beech Woods. Single light bulbs from the roof were transformed into chandeliers and moulded ceilings, and countryside posters on the walls into oak panelling and mounted stags' heads.

Riddlesworth Hall was a splendid place; one of the best money could buy. Diana wasn't the only Honourable as she had been at Silfield, but equally the place wasn't teeming with the junior aristocracy. It was exclusive in as much as it excluded anyone who couldn't afford to pay the fees, which by the 1970s was guaranteed to provide a comprehensive mixture of backgrounds.

The school boasted good facilities, good teachers and an impressive success rate at Common Entrance for public schools like Benenden, Wycombe Abbey, Felixstowe and West Heath.

The day began with a rising bell, actually an old cow bell, rung by the school matron at 7.30 a.m. Once the girls were dressed, those with long hair had to join the hair queue to have it tied back. Diana had fine hair which the matron put into bunches to begin with, and when it grew long enough she wore it in plaits. She always hated the rubber bands but her hair was so fine that there was no other way of keeping it tidy.

Breakfast followed at 8.00 a.m., after which everyone had to go back upstairs to make their own beds, and then get down again and into the senior common room for prayers. They had lessons all morning with a break of half an hour in the middle, which gave them time to drink some milk, eat a biscuit and dash off outside to Pets' Corner to feed their animals.

Pets' Corner was Riddy's brainwave. She believed that allowing girls to care for animals from home was a therapeutic link for the children, and encouraged everyone to bring back some small creature to look after. The result was a menagerie of guinea pigs, rabbits, hamsters and mice, all kept in a shanty town of individual hutches down a yew-lined path known as Ghost Walk.

Once upon a time birds were allowed too, but they proved a little more awkward. A budgie once escaped and was eaten by the cat, and someone else once brought a macaw to school which lived in the senior common room and made irreverent remarks during early morning prayers. It had to go.

But care of the animals was entirely down to the children and, if anyone neglected theirs, it was sent home – although never for very long. Diana brought back her guinea pig called Peanuts, which had won a prize in the previous summer in the local Fur and Feather Show at Sandringham. The following summer she went on to win another prize with him at school: the Palmer Cup for Pets' Corner. She was very fond of Peanuts, and absolutely meticulous about cleaning his cage. She was also quite bossy about the way everyone else looked after their animals, and thoroughly disapproved of anyone who tried to shirk their responsibilities.

Learning to be responsible for them was one advantage of allowing pets at school. There was another. A prospective father was once being shown over the school, and asking rather hesitantly how Miss Ridsdale dealt with the facts of life. At that precise moment a breathless child rushed up to the two of them and said, 'Oh *please* Miss Ridsdale, may I mate my hamster with Sally's?'

Like most schools. Riddlesworth was ruled by bells, from

early morning to lights out at 8.30 p.m. In between, conventional lessons were interspersed with arts and crafts. Everyone learnt pottery, weaving and basketwork as well as drawing and painting.

After lunch there was a rest period. Everyone had to get on to their beds – feet up – with their shoes off and counterpanes off, for forty minutes of silent reading. Not that with ten or twelve children to a dormitory it was ever anything like silent. It was at times like this that the girls would send silly notes to one another, giggle and whisper or pile chairs on top of chests of drawers to write their names high up on the dormitory walls.

Diana's name features more than once about the place: on walls, desks and even on the trees out in the garden. She was no goody-goody. She was always bursting with energy, egging people on to do things, jumping into the swimming pool before the mistress said 'Go', and saying things that would make people giggle at the worst possible moment.

There were games in the afternoons – hockey and netball in winter, tennis and swimming in summer, then more lessons and a half-hour break to see to their animals again before tea and vespers. Every other night they had to have a bath, supervised by the matrons, who kept quite a close eye on things, inspecting wardrobes and drawers regularly, to ensure that they had been tidied every Saturday morning. But tidiness was never a problem for Diana.

There were a few lessons on Saturday mornings too, then church practice in the senior common room where they rehearsed the hymns they would sing in church the following morning. After break they were free until lunchtime; they could go and take their animals out on the lawn, climb trees, or watch for toads in Frogs' Alley outside the gym.

After lunch on both Saturdays and Sundays came the high spot of the week – sweets. It had been democratically decided a long way back by the children that they would rather have a good collection of sweets at the weekends, to take on to their beds with them at rest time, than a measly ration of one sweet every day, and that's the way it stood.

Sweets were kept in tuck boxes in the tuck room, and everyone was allowed either six or eight sweets, to be counted and judged by the matron. It wasn't as simple as it sounds. A Mars bar for instance didn't count the same as a toffee, and it was all laboriously worked out so that no one got more than anyone else – except for those who had strayed from the path of righteousness during the week. They had no sweets, a deterrent far greater than any conventional punishment.

The rest of the afternoon was free. Games were organized if people wanted to play – otherwise they could amuse themselves. Joan Wilkins, known as Wilko, took games, and each day everyone did something. She remembers Diana being fairly keen but by no means fanatical or brilliant – but then Wilko is a self-confessed perfectionist. Diana swam and played netball for her house in inter-house matches. She swam one summer in the school team against Norwich High School, and in her last year she and the rest of the team combined won the Parker Cup for swimming. As a swimmer she had come to the right school. Her other passion was dancing. As well as the ordinary class dancing that everyone did, which included natural movement and Scottish dancing, she took extra ballet lessons which she loved.

This excluded her from riding lessons, which perhaps explains why she never became as keen on horses as her sisters. Ballet and riding could not be combined because for one legs were kept straight, for the other they were bent, and the two positions, if not timetables, clashed. Diana chose ballet.

On Sundays the girls enjoyed a lie-in. The bell didn't go until 8.15 a.m. and there were sausages for breakfast, a great treat. Then there was the solemn business of church in St Peter's just across the courtyard. Everything was done properly. It was Sunday best: hats and coats and gloves and heavy black walking shoes which they all hated having to wear. Before they left they got their collection money from the mistress on duty – three old pennies before decimalization, 5p in Diana's last year – and off they went in a crocodile across the yard to sing hymns they had practised the day before.

Diana's parents used to take it in turns to put in an appearance at Riddlesworth. They never came together, and Diana was always truly delighted to see either. She wasn't of course the only child in the school with divorced parents, but the school was always impressed by the way in which the Althorps handled the situation. They made it easy for her, and never embroiled her in their own problems.

Diana herself never appeared to have any untoward reaction about the drama in her life, although the staff do say that she was never a child to wear her emotions on her sleeve. She was always very controlled, never likely, as they put it, to have 'boo-hooed' under any circumstances.

She usually divided the time she had off in the holidays between her mother and her father at Park House, and always came back apparently having enjoyed herself. She was light-hearted, cheerful and even-tempered.

Between church and lunch on Sunday everyone had to write their letters home. Diana always wrote to both her father and mother once a week, although sometimes the second one would go off on a Thursday, which was another period set aside for letter writing. What she wrote was private; the staff read letters to friends, but never those to parents.

Roast Sunday lunch was followed by an extra long rest, taken with a fistful of sweets again, after which all the girls were turned out in their wellington boots on to the heath behind the school for an hour and a half's walk, supervised by the matron.

This was no orderly crocodile that progressed up past Goose Girl's Cottage to One Tree Hill. With one hundred and twenty girls to two matrons, and sometimes one, it was more like the Charge of the Light Brigade through the heather; but in the wilds of Norfolk there was no one to disturb.

The grounds at Riddlesworth and the heath behind were a little girl's paradise, with trees that might have been specially made for making houses. Near the house there was Climbing Cedar and Big Cedar, which the children all believed were protecting it. Further away was Little Beech Wood, and away up in Big Beech Wood was a tree called Shippy, which was perfect for 'Jam Rolls' – they rolled over the branch and dropped off onto the ground.

Many a headmistress would doubtless have banned tree climbing for fairly obvious reasons – there were bound to be casualties – but as this very wise headmistress saw it: 'They were going to climb trees anyway, and I didn't wish them to risk their necks by scrambling down too hurriedly when they saw me coming.' Diana didn't ever break anything on the trees. Her bouts in the sick room were to isolate infectious diseases like mumps and chicken pox.

Riddy remembers desperately trying to keep Lord Althorp away one time because when challenged he had confessed to her that he hadn't had mumps himself, but he wasn't so easily put off. He arrived to see his lumpy-faced daughter sitting up in bed in a room full of lumpy-faced companions, bearing a large basket of fruit, not just for her, but for all the girls in the sick room.

'He was marvellous,' said Riddy, echoing Miss Lowe's opinion from Silfield School. 'I have nothing but admiration for him.' Other members of staff lauded him too: 'Such a nice man. Always very caring and anxious to do the best thing for her.' 'Interested in how she was getting on, and whether she was happy.'

Diana was happy. After her initial homesickness and misery, she forgot herself and was overtaken by the busyness of the place. She became her old self, alive and full of go, always wanting to dash on to the next thing. She had a number of friends, no one in particular, and unlike so many people who lose touch with friends from their pre-teen days, she has kept in contact with a lot of them. But she was never a leader: always happy to fit in with what was going; all the qualities that make for a popular schoolgirl. Not the sort of girl the others looked up to, but the sort they liked to have around. She was a girl who wanted to be liked.

At the end of her first year she won the Legatt Cup for helpfulness, for volunteering to do things around the school. From a behavioural point of view she was a teacher's dream: well-mannered, eager to please, friendly, pleasant, even-tempered and always co-operative.

Academically she got by. No one pretends she was bright. But equally they say she wasn't dull either. The unanimous verdict from teachers and contemporaries alike is that she 'had lots of common sense', which has probably stood her in better stead for the hurdles she had to come, and even the future she still has before her, than a lot of exam passes might have done.

During the autumn term at Riddlesworth in 1972, Diana's Spencer grandmother died, which upset her enormously. She had always been very fond of Cynthia – everyone who knew old Countess Spencer was fond of her – and in the years since her mother had gone Diana had become quite close to her. Many people say that Diana's own qualities and her ease with children are inherited from this grandmother.

Of all the Spencer children, only Sarah went to the memorial service in Northampton that December. The rest, Diana included, were given special permission to take time off school for the official memorial service in London, at the Chapel Royal in St James's Palace, held at the end of January. The Queen Mother was also there, as were Princess Margaret and the Duchess of Gloucester.

In the summer of 1973, Diana took her Common Entrance and was accepted by West Heath, a small select boarding school near Sevenoaks in Kent, which her two sisters had attended.

Sarah, by this time had been unceremoniously ejected for misdemeanours; a disappointing end to an otherwise promising school career. She had passed six 'O' levels, she had been in all the school plays, she had passed Grade V on the piano, and ridden in the senior school team at Hickstead. But Sarah was bored, and was duly advised that she might take her lacrosse stick and her trunk and kiss her friends goodbye.

Jane had taken over where Sarah had left off. She had passed eleven 'O' levels by the time Diana arrived, had been in the tennis team and the lacrosse team, and was now a prefect and working up to 'A' levels. So one way and another, Diana had quite some reputation to follow when she arrived there in September 1973.

West Heath was founded in 1865 by the Reverend P. B. Power, 'late incumbent of Christ Church, Worthing', and Mrs Power, who wanted to 'receive a few Young Ladies whose education would be conducted on religious principles, with that of their own Daughters'. It was originally started in a small house in Abbey Wood, Kent, but then moved to Ham

Common, and finally in 1932 to its present site, a magnificent country house in thirty-two acres of farm and woodland near Sevenoaks.

Girls hoping for a place all sit the Common Entrance exam, but there is no pass or fail mark. The only qualification they need, apart from having enough money to pay the fees, is an ability to express themselves neatly and tidily on paper, all the old-fashioned things, as the Principal says, which go with a willingness to share what they have.

Miss Ruth Rudge has been principal for the last sixteen years, and a Latin teacher in the school for almost double that. She is a tall, straightforward woman with a wry sense of humour. She is known by the girls as Ruth or Rudge and runs a happy house – like Riddlesworth it seems to be more of an extended family than a school. The children are not always academically stretched. There is a stronger accent on music than on exams – but they thrive, have lots of friends, and all come away with the impression that you can't be anything but happy at West Heath because it's so small.

Diana was no exception. She settled in better than many of her contemporaries because as well as having her sister Jane in the school and her cousin Diana Wake-Walker, she had the added advantage of already having been a boarder at Riddlesworth. Besides, how could anyone feel miserable in a school that calls its dormitories by the names of flowers and its forms by the names of trees? Which particular dormitories Diana slept in during her four years no one can remember – but she left her mark in two. The unmistakably rounded hand of Diana Spencer is inscribed on the inside of the cupboards in both Delphinium and Cowslip for posterity. And as at Riddlesworth, what at the time would have been a punishable offence is now the subject of a certain amount of glee.

Diana started off in a form called Poplar. Girls were put into forms according to age, but were then put into divisions for work according to ability. So it was not impossible to be in a division for a subject you were good at with girls two forms above, and, for a subject you were weak at, with girls from forms below. There were usually no more than eight people in each division.

51

Here, as before, Diana was not very good academically. She came out of the school after four years and on term with no exam passes whatsoever. Quite an achievement, some would say. But the emphasis wasn't on exams. Miss Rudge herself once said of their aims:

What we remember from school are rather the people we met there, the teachers themselves rather than their lessons. The training in the art of living together is the most important part of school-life: the endless variety of experiences including squabbles, accusations, sharing or lack of sharing, clashes of personalities, together with much mutual joy and helpfulness between those of the same and of different generations are the experiences that form attitudes and judgements, and teach tolerance or leave us with a sense of frustration that will affect our lives and our relationships with others far more than the acquisition of three 'A' levels and six 'O' levels.

I am sure that in the long run, it is one's own consciousness of the dignity and the importance of oneself to others, and the awareness of others as individuals with problems similar to one's own, and the knowledge of how to cope with oneself and with others in the endless variety of situations in which one finds oneself, that are of prime importance in living. This I hope we are learning here, and if so our existence is justified.

Miss Rudge says academic subjects were 'not Diana's forte' but equally she wasn't 'a no-hoper'. She was an all-round average.

She is certainly not as stupid as her failure to pass any exams would indicate. Her friends say the real reason she failed to get any 'O' levels was sheer laziness and the fact that she was never pushed.

One of her close friends at school planned exactly the same sort of career for herself with children, sat exactly the same subjects as Diana in the same term, and failed the lot too. 'We just used to spend all our time reading Barbara Cartland books, really awful romantic slush novels, when we were supposed to be doing prep,' she said. 'We read hundreds of them. We had a craze on them. We all used to buy as many as we could in the holidays and sneak them back in, and we'd swap them around.'

Diana's other problem was that exams made her panic.

When confronted with a blank sheet of paper in the deathly hush of a GCE examination room, she forgot everything she ever knew bar her name. So when she sat down to her exams in June 1977, English Language, English Literature, Art and Geography, she failed the lot. Some of her friends who had failed left at the end of the summer and went on to do re-takes in sixth form colleges elsewhere. Diana chose to stay on at West Heath and re-take the exams in the autumn, but she was no more successful second time around and left that Christmas.

Diana melded into the life and the routine of the school perfectly. She had plenty of friends, but no particular best friend. Miss Rudge discouraged it. 'I disapprove of girls having best friends,' she explained. 'They are bound to break up and have traumas, and they don't get involved in what everyone else is doing. I think it's very limiting to a child if all their attention is on another child, both emotionally and from the point of view of socializing.'

At the end of each term she would call each girl into her study to see her individually, and they would discuss the girl's work, the staff reports on how they had done, any problems they might have, and who they would like to share a room with the following term. She reasoned that it was pointless putting them in with people they wouldn't get on with. But they could never choose to be with the same person two terms running, because that might encourage a special friendship.

Diana never slept with any furry bears or animals on her bed. All she had to remind her of home was an array of photographs of her family, her animals and Park House on the chest of drawers by her bed.

The first bell of the morning, the rising bell, rang at 7.30 a.m. for breakfast at 8 o'clock sharp. A few girls had baths then, but most had them in the evening on a rota, each girl being allocated a bath three times a week. Hairwashing was once a week, supervised initially by Mrs Allen, the matron.

Diana was a compulsive washer. She couldn't let a day go by without having a bath, no matter how late it was. She would sometimes sneak into the bathroom after lights out and wash herself while the water was still running, then jump out and pull the plug. And she washed her hair illegally too, in between the official weekly washes. She also had a compulsion about washing clothes. Girls were allowed to wash bras, pants and socks, but had to get permission from the matron to wash anything bigger because of the shortage of drying space in the linen room. The larger items were supposed to be sent to the laundry and the girls made their own lists each week. Diana sought permission more than most people to do extra washing.

And when she went away for the weekend – girls were allowed two off each term plus a half-term exeat of four days – Diana used to go to stay with either of her sisters in London and do their washing for them and generally clean up their flats.

Breakfast was eaten downstairs in the oak-panelled dining room where the girls sat twelve to a table, a mixture of ages with a prefect at the head of each. There was cereal, something cooked – as often as not baked beans – then bread and marmalade, and tea in a jug on each table. On Sundays there was coffee. The only stipulation at breakfast was that everyone had to eat something. The problems of anorexia loomed large at West Heath as at every other girls' boarding school, although this was never any problem at that time for Diana. She loved food, particularly baked beans, and she'd help herself to anything up to four bowls of All-Bran every morning. But she did put on weight easily and periodically had to slow down on the baked beans.

After breakfast they all went upstairs to make their beds, which had to be stripped back before breakfast, then go down to their form rooms to get the post and collect their hymn books ready for prayers at three minutes to nine. The early morning post was one of the high spots of the day. A prefect used to bring the letters round to each form room inside a folded copy of the *Daily Telegraph*. Diana's letters were mostly from her family. Prince Andrew never wrote to her, as people have suggested. She didn't get letters from boyfriends at all for the simple reason she didn't have any. None of the girls had boyfriends at that time, although they all liked to talk. Diana was always very keen to be first with the newspaper. She loved reading it, particularly the Court Circular and the fashion pages.

The girls were allowed to wear home clothes at the weekend, and one of Miss Rudge's most vivid memories of Diana was the way she dressed, in particular in a pair of bright red dungarees. 'The way she dresses now is just an extension of the way she dressed here. She had a sense of colour. She was meticulous about the way she looked. It was natural to her – she's a neat, tidy person, and simple. She always dressed simply, but there was a bit of distinction about her even if she was wearing jeans and doing the weeding.'

The weeding was Ruth's pet punishment, inflicted on anyone caught talking after lights out, running in the passageway past the kitchens, or storing chocolate in their sock drawers. She herself enjoyed gardening, she said she liked the company – also someone else to do the hard work. But there were other tasks to perform, such as polishing the brass in the entrance hall, cleaning the baths over the weekend, or sweeping the passageways when there were no cleaning staff to do it.

Diana pulled out her fair share of thistles in her four years at West Heath. 'She wasn't good all the time and she wasn't bad all the time. She was a perfectly ordinary girl.'

The day began with prayers held in the school hall where a hymn was sung, prayers said, and Ruth read out any notices for the day. Towards the end of every term the hymns were chosen by the girls who were leaving at the end of that term. The one Diana chose when she left at the end of the autumn term in 1977 was 'I Vow To Thee My Country' – the very same hymn she chose at her wedding in St Paul's Cathedral.

Lessons began after prayers and the girls moved from room to room for lessons, carrying their books in canvas or PVC carrier bags. Woe betide anyone who left a book behind or a jumper hanging over the back of a chair. It would be 'conked', confiscated, and only returnable on payment of a fine. The money collected from 'conks' went towards buying materials to make up into nightdresses and bedjackets for old people, which would then be taken to Queen Mary's Needlework Guild and distributed to charity. Queen Mary had been a pupil at West Heath in the 1880s, when she was Princess May of Teck.

Diana was never much good at needlework, a compulsory

subject, or maths, and was worse still at French. But then she had never had the opportunity, like so many of the girls in the school, to practise it. When term was over and the holidays came, Diana never went abroad: she didn't go to the South of France in summer or ski in winter. She had never even been in an aeroplane. Her holidays were spent at home, with either her father or her mother. Soon after Countess Spencer's death, Diana's mother and stepfather moved hundreds of miles away to Scotland, near Oban, off the west coast, and Diana had yet another 'home' to go to for half of the holiday.

This one was a far cry from the manicured parkland at Sandringham. It wasn't grand; it was a white-washed working farmhouse, set on a wild, windy hillside, where it rained three hundred and sixty-four days of the year, and everyone lived in jeans.

Diana loved it, and often used to take friends from school up to stay with her there. She spent a lot of her time walking on both the island and the mainland, despite the rain. She used to go out in Peter's boat to put down lobster pots with him, or go fishing for mackerel, or simply for a trip up and down the coast. She helped her mother get her Shetland ponies ready to show, helped occasionally in the shop she ran, and in the summer holidays even braved the freezing Atlantic for a swim.

But she was never sorry to have to go back to Park House for Johnnie's share of her holiday. That was her real home; she loved it. She had her animals there, and there was the park to walk in and friends nearby. She didn't have friends in the other places where she spent her holidays – not surprisingly, for she was never there long enough.

Back at school, if Diana didn't shine in the classroom, she did better at games, which were played every afternoon from 2.00 to 3.00 p.m. – lacrosse, hockey and netball in winter, tennis and swimming in summer. She was in the hockey team at one point, and also the lacrosse team – known as lax – although she never did as well as her sister Jane who was consistently in the team, won her colours for lacrosse and was at one time captain of the First XII.

The summer term was Diana's favourite for sports. She was never in the team but she loved tennis – there are four hard courts and eight grass at West Heath – and she used to play in her own time in the evenings for pleasure. She has even been heard to say that she hopes to wean Charles off racing and interest him in playing tennis; although the baby will have let him off the hook for a bit.

Summer meant swimming too, which was her forte. Diana was more at home in water than anywhere. In her first summer she won the Junior Swimming Sports, in her second year the Junior Swimming Cup, in her third year she got her colours and won the Senior Swimming Cup and a Diving Cup, and in her last summer she had her colours renewed.

Swimming officially only took place in the summer. It was an outdoor pool, although heated, and in the winter months it was left uncovered with tyres floating on the water to stop ice forming and cracking the walls. There was one occasion, however, on which Diana climbed in with the tyres. One freezing cold afternoon in November, in the dark, she was dared to swim two widths of the pool. The water was green and slimy and ice-cold, but much to the admiration and astonishment of the friends who had dared her, she did climb in and swim two widths.

Diana never smoked at school – which, had she been caught, would have got her smartly expelled – nor drank gin in the rhododendrons in true St Trinian's style. She wasn't interested in either. Food was much more of a temptation. Ruth didn't allow extra food or sweets. As she reasoned with the girls, it was something that could so easily get out of hand. Some people would be able to afford far more than others and she didn't want this kind of competition going on at school.

There was one exception to the rule. My Taylor, an English master, used to sell chocolate bars twice a week in one of the form rooms. He bought them cheaply at the Cash and Carry and sold them at normal shop prices; the profit he made was divided up between school funds and the donkey sanctuary.

Despite the odd Mars bar from him, Diana and her friends always felt half starved, and used to slip away into Sevenoaks in the afternoons to stock up on sweets. She had a particular passion for cream eggs.

It was in Sevenoaks, at a little place called Adam and Eve,

that Diana had her ears pierced. It was another craze that was going round the school and to begin with she wore gold studs in her ears. Studs or sleepers were the only sort of jewellery that was officially allowed, although Ruth didn't enforce the rule rigidly. Diana always used to wear a fine silver bracelet with hearts on it, a gold Russian wedding ring on her little finger, and the letter D on a chain round her neck which her friends clubbed together and gave her as a birthday present one year. It was the same D she was wearing in the early photographs of her taken at the kindergarten in Pimlico and when the engagement was first announced.

Diana's birthday on 1 July always fell during the school term, but presents were actually discouraged by Ruth, on the same grounds as the food rule – the pressure of competition on some girls who wouldn't be able to afford as much as others. Girls were only allowed to have parties in the two bottom forms, Cedar and Poplar, and then only in the summer term when they could be held out-of-doors. But Diana did have one more birthday party in her last summer at West Heath. It doubled as a leaving party for the whole year, after 'O' levels had been taken – but before the results. There were twenty-five people in the year, and they took themselves and a mound of food and drink down to a field above Gracious Lane Bridge for the afternoon. Everyone had contributed food, and there was a feast: chicken pieces, a brace of pheasant, shrimps, prawns, cakes, biscuits and crisps, and plenty of Coca Cola and lemonade and orange juice to drink – some still for Diana because she hated fizzy drinks. They had a glorious afternoon, and what they didn't eat they flung at each other.

Other afternoons in her last year were spent rather more respectably. Once a week she used to visit an old lady living near Sevenoaks with another girl from the school, both members of the Voluntary Service Unit. It simply involved sitting down, chatting for an hour or two, and making tea, or helping with anything the old lady couldn't do alone.

At weekends Diana very often used to go out with her two sisters. Sarah had been away to a finishing school in Switzerland after leaving West Heath, and had taken a secretarial course, but was now in London living in a flat, and was working for Savill's, the estate agents. Being an old girl, albeit not one of the school's most fêted old girls, she was allowed to come down on any weekend during the term and take Diana out to lunch or tea on a Saturday or Sunday, which ordinary friends or relatives could only do on a set number of days, and Jane followed suit once she left.

When Diana's parents visited her they came separately – the only time they both appeared was for her confirmation. Neither ever came to a garden party, or a school play, or sports day with their new partners. Instead, they would bring Sarah and Jane and Charles too, if he was around.

On other weekends, a school group went off on outings, to exhibitions, concerts, museums or to the theatre or the ballet. Diana always put her name down for expeditions to the ballet, to the Coliseum or Sadler's Wells. She saw *Swan Lake* at least four times, also *Giselle*, *Coppelia*, and *The Sleeping Beauty*. She adored ballet and cherished dreams of dancing professionally herself, but she was too tall.

Nevertheless, she took extra ballet lessons, as she had done at Riddlesworth, and also learnt tap and ballroom dancing. Her teacher was a girl called Wendy Vickers who had been trained by Betty Vacani, niece and partner of the late Marguerite Vacani, who between them have taught three generations of royal children to dance.

Diana loved her dancing and worked at it hard, sometimes practising before breakfast. This paid dividends, for she won the school dancing competition at the end of the spring term in 1976, which was judged by Miss Vacani herself.

While she was at West Heath Diana also took up the piano which, curiously, she had never played before, despite her grandmother's passion for it. Her sisters both played. Jane had reached Grade III in the Associated Board of the Royal Schools of Music exams, and Sarah had taken and passed Grade V by the time she was fifteen. Diana didn't start until she was fourteen, and although she never got any grades she had talent. According to Miss Rudge, 'for someone who started late she made phenomenal progress. Everyone wished that she'd begun to play earlier.' She would practise in the music corridor, a succession of small rooms with upright pianos in them set aside from the main building.

Diana's friends at West Heath were people like Caroline Harbord-Hammond, with whom she had been at Riddlesworth, Theresa Mowbray who was her mother's goddaughter and whom she saw out of term time too, Mary-Ann Stewart-Richardson who also lived in Norfolk, and Sarah Robeson, who shared her interest in children. She and Sarah both planned to work with children when they left school, and both were to do so. While they were at West Heath they used to look after the English master's children in their free time. Mr Smallwood was married to an Italian and lived in a cottage in the grounds. Sarah and Diana would go across after games in the afternoons and take his two children, who spoke only Italian, out for a walk in the woods.

Sarah and Diana were also always the first in the dining room at supper time. They used to go into the kitchen ten minutes early and help Barbara, who worked in the pantry, to take the dishes from the hatch, wheel them on a trolley into the dining room, and distribute them to the tables. This wasn't pure love of either food or work. There was cunning in their ardour. This way at supper they got seats which were close to the door, so that they could get out quickly at the weekends and get the comfortable chairs in the common room to watch television.

They always sat glued to the old films on a Sunday afternoon. Diana loved anything romantic. She also liked programmes such as *The Generation Game*, *Crossroads* and *Charlie's Angels*. She would have been at school watching the last about the same time as Prince Charles was also enjoying Charlie's Angels – in real life. One of the stars of the series, Farrah Fawcett-Majors, was one of the many beautiful women whom Charles is said to have taken a passing fancy to in his time.

Diana was also inseparable from the television during Wimbledon fortnight, and every year her mother would arrange tickets for the first Saturday. After lessons ended at lunchtime on Saturday morning she would change into home clothes and dash off to be there for the start of play at 2 p.m.

The main feature of Sunday was church at St Mary's in

Kippington, one and a half miles down the road. There were two services, one at 8 a.m. and one at 11 a.m. Those not yet confirmed went to the 11 a.m. service and the only means of getting there and back was on foot, which tended to take up the whole morning. But there were compensations in going to 'late' service – a lie in. Breakfast wasn't until 9 a.m., in order to give time to the older girls who had been at 8 o'clock to get back. Moreover, it was special breakfast on Sundays: hot rolls, a boiled egg and coffee.

Diana was confirmed on 12 March 1976, when she was fifteen, by the Bishop of Rochester at Kippington, having been prepared by Canon John Rahe-Hughes, who happened to be holding the fort that year in between vicars. Her mother and father both came to the ceremony, also her sisters and a smattering of godparents.

Thereafter she could go to early service on a Sunday morning, and have the rest of the morning free to read the Sunday papers and Barbara Cartland novels, write letters to home or do her washing.

In her last term Diana was made a prefect – something she had never been at Riddlesworth – unusual since she was leaving at Christmas. Ruth usually only made prefects of girls who were staying on the whole year. That entitled her to move out of the main building and sleep in the post 'O' level study bedroom known as 'Cowsheds'. It was so called for obvious reasons. It consisted of one long corridor with partitions on either side, each one housing a bed, a desk and a chest of drawers. But there was a kitchenette at one end and a certain amount of privacy and independence.

In that last term when, she was retaking her 'O' levels, she also won the Miss Clark Lawrence Award for service to the school, which is not always given. It's 'for anyone who has done things that otherwise might have gone unsung,' explains Ruth. 'And I remember her telling me that winning it was one of the most surprising things that had ever happened to her.'

A NEW ORDER

ALTHOUGH LIFE at school had continued happily and securely, life at home had changed dramatically in the previous year, and Diana's fragile world had been turned upside down. On 9 June 1975, Diana's grandfather had died aged eighty-three. This was upsetting news itself, broken to her and her cousin, Diana Wake-Walker, after prayers one morning by their headmistress. Diana was further upset that her father couldn't have told her himself.

With the old Earl's death the family lost a whole way of life: Johnnie became the 8th Earl and inherited Althorp; Sarah, Jane and Diana all became Ladies; and Charles became Viscount Althorp at the age of eleven. That summer they moved lock, stock and barrel from their friendly corner of Norfolk by the sea to the splendours of a stately home in Northamptonshire.

When Diana arrived home from school at the end of that summer term Park House was in the midst of being packed up ready for the move. There were boxes and packing cases everywhere, and Diana couldn't bear to watch; so she rang up Alex Loyd, raided the larder in the house of all its peaches, and they went off to the beach hut at Brancaster for the day and sat and ate the lot. It was the last time she ever went there.

Althorp presented a whole new way of life. Park House may have been bleak from the outside, but inside it was a comfortable family home. Althorp was a vast stately home, steeped in family history and containing one of the finest private art collections in Europe. Diana had known the house when she was younger. Her father never went there while his father was alive, although Frances had made an effort to take the children across to Althorp periodically. But that had been before Frances left home, eight years before, so Diana's memory of the house was very slight.

She certainly had no friends in Northampton, and although there was a tennis court, there was no swimming pool at the house, and it couldn't have been further from the sea. Her father soon remedied that and built a swimming pool, but Diana never grew to be fond of the place.

This was partly because along with the move to Althorp came a yet more dramatic change in Diana's life. Shortly before his father's death, Johnnie had been somewhat reconciled to the old man via the new woman in his life, Raine, Countess of Dartmouth, the flamboyant, outspoken daughter of Diana's favourite authoress, Barbara Cartland.

Raine and Johnnie had been working together on a book she was writing for the Greater London Council called *What Is Our Heritage?* Johnnie, always a keen photographer, was taking the pictures for the book, and they fell in love.

Raine was forty-six; she had been married to the Earl of Dartmouth for twenty-eight years and had four children by him. Worse still, Dartmouth, when he was plain Gerald Legge, had been a close friend of Johnnie's at Eton.

The affair caused ructions all round. Her mother, Barbara Cartland, who had been writing fiction about romances like this since time immemorial, was shocked to the core, but stood by her daughter. 'She came to see me and said "Mummy, I'm madly in love, just like one of your heroines." What can you do? You've got to stand by your daughter.' Her husband was equally shocked, but he divorced Raine and took custody of their four children, William, Rupert, Charlotte and Henry, although the two eldest were grown up by then.

Johnnie's children – Sarah, Jane, Diana and Charles – were not so much shocked as horrified. Raine was a formidable woman. As one of her friends put it, 'She's not a person, she's an experience'; and as a former colleague on the GLC observed: 'Raine has an iron hand in an iron glove which is so beautifully wrought that people don't realize even the glove is made of iron until it hits them.' But this sort of charm worked wonders on the old Earl who was flattered by her attentions.

Raine, whose maiden name had been McCorquodale, had been in the public eye for years. She was seldom out of the gossip columns. As Lady Lewisham she had been a forceful member of the Westminster City Council, the London County Council and the Greater London Council, and was constantly sounding off about any controversial subject from refuse collection to cracked cups at London Airport and smutty films. In fighting to stop the film *Ulysses* being shown, she didn't let the fact that she hadn't seen it get in her way. 'It's an absolutely revolting book,' she said, dismissing further discussion, 'and it must be a revolting film.' But she was also a clever woman. Underneath the exotic plumage lay a determined lady, who took on and took over Althorp and all who lived there.

She and Johnnie were married on 14 July 1976 at Caxton Hall in London, with only two witnesses, one of whom was her half-brother Glen McCorquodale. No one else knew. By the time they did, she was installed as mistress of Althorp, and had set about putting the Spencer house in order. It has to be said to her credit, however, that the only reason the estate is a going concern today is because of Raine's business sense. Had she not taken a very forceful hand and brought a touch of brutal reality into the running of the house, it would in all probability have been taken over by the National Trust years ago. There were crippling duties to pay after the 7th Earl died, and Johnnie wouldn't have known where to begin on his own.

It wasn't just the house that Raine took over. She dominated Johnnie, and she tried her best to take over his children too. But they were not children to be taken over. They had never come across a woman like this – few people have – and in the end the two elder girls preferred to stay away; away from Althorp and away from their father.

They could no longer sit over dinner and have his attention, share confidences with him, and seek his advice as they had done in the past. They had to compete with Raine; and it must have been a puzzle to him that his children didn't share his enthusiasm for his new wife.

The bitterest battles were between Raine and the two eldest daughters, Sarah and Jane, aged twenty and eighteen respectively when she became their step-mother in July 1976. In an interview with Jean Rook of the *Daily Express* shortly after Diana's engagement Raine admitted they hadn't got on.

It was bloody awful [she said]. And all right, for the first time I'm going to say my piece because I'm absolutely sick of the Wicked Stepmother lark. You're never going to make me sound like a human being, because people like to think I'm Dracula's mother, but I did have a rotten time at the start and it's only just getting better.

Sarah resented me, even my place at the head of the table, and gave orders to the servants over my head. Jane didn't speak to me for two years, even if we bumped in a passageway.

Diana was sweet, always did her own thing.

Becoming a step-mother is an unenviable role for any woman but Raine could have handled the children with more tact. She was after all walking into a family that had had no mother for eight years, and who were used to being the centre of their father's attention. And they were scarcely children. Sarah and Jane both had flats in London, with jobs and friends and lives of their own. Diana was fourteen, and away at school at West Heath for most of the year, but on weekends off she would very often go and stay with either Sarah or Jane in London. When she did go home she let it all wash over her with more success than the others.

Over the years the difficulties and differences settled down, and they all learned to live with Raine on the occasions when they came to Althorp, but none of the children ever became close to her. They were simply not the same type, and the plans that she had for their family home would have made their grandfather reel in his grave.

When Sarah was first asked, soon after they moved, why Lady Dartmouth was spending so much time at Althorp she replied rather icily: 'She is helping my father open the house on a commercial basis. In my grandfather's time he did not care for the idea of the public walking around his house. Lady Dartmouth is writing a guide for it with my father.'

The new Countess Spencer was doing more than writing a guide. She was pruning the staff and the household budget to a minimum. Old retainers were retired. New staff came in their place. But where there had been a full complement of servants in Jack Spencer's day there was now no more than the barest minimum; a cook, a housemaid, a butler and a ladies' maid.

The west wing was appointed to the family. The rest of the house was smartened up and put on display, and the paying public walked in. The stable block, built to the same design as

St Paul's church in Covent Garden, was turned into a tea room, a souvenir shop, and in another section a wine shop. And coachloads of day-trippers arrived in ever increasing numbers.

Everything had come from Park House when the family moved, including such animals as were left by then: Marmalade the cat, the dog, a gitshound called Gitsy, Hammy – a hamster, no less, who escaped and everyone suspects was eaten by the dog – and a collection of Java sparrows which belonged to Charles. But none of them got much further than the staff hall.

While Park House had been big by most people's standards, it was nevertheless a cosy, family, lived-in sort of place. Althorp was enormous, and every bit the stately home: vast rooms with high moulded ceilings, chandeliers, gracious fireplaces and marble floors; fine antique furniture, priceless paintings, rare books, tapestries, precious porcelain, and sculpture. It's not surprising that Diana liked to go and sit on top of the Aga in the kitchen from time to time.

All the children had their own bedrooms, and all still have, except for Jane who lives in a house in the grounds. Diana's bedroom was the old night nursery on the first floor, with its own bathroom, near to her father's suite of rooms. It had two single beds, a bookshelf filled with Barbara Cartland novels, and a sofa with all Diana's soft toys sitting neatly lined up on it. The walls were cream, the curtains cream and brown and the floor covered in linoleum, with rugs thrown over to add a bit of creature comfort. But after two boarding schools, Diana was used to a minimum.

The staff at Althorp all loved her. In contrast to her step-mother, she would dress in jeans, saunter into the kitchen if she felt peckish, chatter to the cook, even the man delivering the groceries, if he happened to turn up while she was about. She never asked or expected anyone to treat her like a lady. She was warm, friendly and chatty to everyone. She even did all her own washing and ironing when she came to the house, and her brother's too.

She wore no make-up, and spent her days swimming – in summer, literally all day – walking in the park and dancing. She used to dance in the entrance hall, officially the Wootton

The ties between the Spencers and the Royal Family have always been close. This photograph was taken during a visit by Queen Mary to the Spencer home at Althorp. From left: Lady Cynthia, Countess Spencer, Lady Anne Spencer, Queen Mary, 7th Earl Spencer, and Viscount Althorp, who was to become Diana's father

Left: Johnnie Althorp's marriage to Frances Roche in Westminster Abbey in 1954 was the Society wedding of the year. The page boys were dressed in white satin suits with blue sashes, copied from Reynolds' portrait of Lord Althorp, which hangs in the Marlborough Room at Althorp. Above: Frances, aged sixteen, with her mother, Ruth, Lady Fermoy. Below: Park House on the Sandringham estate in Norfolk, where Diana was born and spent the first fourteen years of her life

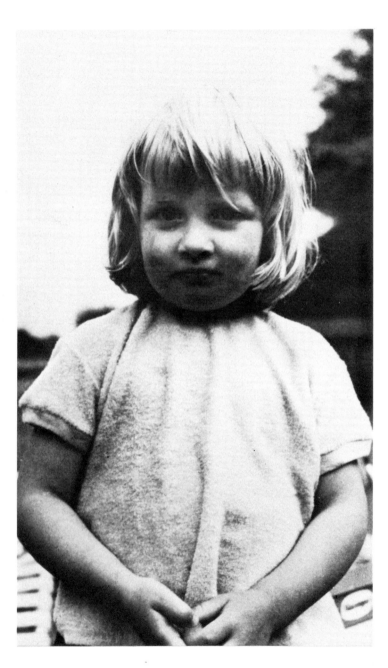

Left: Diana, aged three, at Park House. Right: Diana was never short of attention as a baby. Her sisters, six-year-old Sarah and Jane, aged four, took great pride in showing her off to the locals at Sandringham. Below: Diana with her brother Charles at their Uncle Edmund Fermoy's house in Berkshire

Above: Diana, second from left, with her class-mates at Silfield School in King's Lynn. Below: The swimming pool that Johnnie had built for his children a Park House

Above: In June 1975 Johnnie became the 8th Earl Spencer, master of Althorp and one of the wealthiest landowners in England. Below: Sarah and Diana Spencer at their sister Jane's wedding. Diana was one of the bridesmaids

The photograph that will go down in history, and the last time that Diana wore her skirt without a petticoat. Diana is with two of the children from the Young England Kindergarten

Hall, on the black and white marbled floor which was perfect for tap. She would set herself up with a portable record player, shut all the doors – she would never dance if anyone was watching – start the music and dance for hours.

She doubtless thought nothing of using one of the set of priceless mahogany chairs backed with the family coat of arms as a practice bar for ballet, pirouetting past the bust of David Garrick, the famous actor who spent Christmas in the house in 1778, and practising her three-quarter frappés under the scrutiny of previous Lord Spencers on the walls and black Roman figures fished out of the River Tiber and given to the great Duke of Marlborough by General Charles Churchill. But that, of course, was strictly out of visiting hours. The Wootton Hall is the first room the public are shown into on their conducted tour of the house.

Her step-mother's lifestyle couldn't have been more different. Raine actually disliked the country and was far happier spending time in the Spencer flat in London, or down at her flat in Brighton. When she was at Althorp she might just as well have been closeted in Eaton Mews for all the country air she took. She spent her mornings in bed, where she would do all her work of the day; sitting in splendour beneath a pile of files and papers that were strewn out all over the bedclothes, making it impossible for her to move without disturbing them all.

When Raine was up she dressed immaculately, always in suits and high-heeled shoes, looking very much the part of a Countess. In the evenings she would dress for dinner every night in a long gown, even when she and Johnnie were the only people in the house. When Diana came to stay, she was expected to put on a long dress in the evenings too, although during the day she lived in jeans, or jumpers and skirts.

Whatever Diana may have thought of her step-mother, she was always very kind to Raine's younger children, Charlotte who was fourteen when Raine married Johnnie, and Henry who was only eight. Custody was given to Lord Dartmouth, so they didn't live at Althorp permanently, but came, as she herself did, for part of their holidays.

Another member of Raine's family that came to Althorp periodically was her mother, that vision of pink frills and feathers. Barbara Cartland who, in between proclaiming the wonders of natural honey, vitamin E3 and ginseng, had written almost as many romantic novels as there are days in the year, most of which Diana had read.

It was about the time when Diana was sitting down to her 'O' level exams, in June 1977, that Sarah had unwittingly begun to map the future for her youngest sister.

She had met Prince Charles at Ascot, and the two of them had hit it off very well together. She became his latest girl-friend, and for the next seven months was touted as a possible bride.

The British press had been in such a frenzy for years to marry him off, that any girl seen with him, and a few that had never been seen with him, were rashly hailed as the future Queen of England.

When Sarah met the Prince she was suffering from the slimmers' disease anorexia nervosa, and he is said to have helped her through it. Whether or not he did, she went into hospital for treatment six weeks after their first meeting, and six months later was very much better.

For a while between Diana's engagement and the announcement that she was pregnant, during which time she lost nearly two stone in weight, there was speculation, repeated after the birth of Prince William, that she may have been suffering from anorexia nervosa too. She had all the qualifications: there is no totally common denominator in those who are affected, but it is usually girls aged between eighteen and twenty, often from middle-class backgrounds, who are generally highly strung or have had some trauma in their lives – and neither Sarah nor Diana was lacking that. Anorexics stop eating in order to become slim and once slim find they no longer have the desire to eat again, either physically or mentally. They go to elaborate lengths to avoid eating, they lie about it, they invent stories. Some, if unable to avoid eating, do eat, then make themselves sick immediately afterwards. Very often they become so thin that they lose their monthly periods and as a result have difficulty in becoming pregnant. Some die. It generally takes a psychiatrist to cure someone with anorexia.

Sarah was cured, and for the rest of that year she and

Charles saw a lot of each other, apart from the period in the autumn when Charles went off on an American tour.

In November he went to spend a night at Althorp, as Sarah's guest, to shoot on the estate the following day. That was the day on which Sarah, as she later said, 'played Cupid', the day on which Diana and Charles met for the first time that either could remember, in the middle of a ploughed field at Nobottle Wood. But Diana was only sixteen then, home from boarding school for the weekend, and no one thought any more of it at the time.

The next month, December 1977, Diana left school after failing her 'O' levels for the second time, and after Christmas she went to Switzerland, to the finishing school that Sarah had attended, the Institut Alpin Videmanette at Château d'Oex near Gstaad.

When she arrived in Switzerland, Diana was sixteen and a half; it was the first time she had been away from all her friends and her family in her life, the first time she had been in an aeroplane and the first time she had been abroad. She was thrown into a school year that was already in progress – most girls stayed from September until July, therefore they all knew one another – into a group of sixty, of whom only nine were English-speaking, and told that if she dared to break the rules and speak anything but French, she would be punished.

Diana's French had never been good at school, and she was understandably miserable. As it happens, she quickly made friends with the English girls and one in particular, Sophie Kimball, became a close friend. Despite the rules she talked English almost exclusively during her few weeks there, and she was still bitterly homesick.

In theory she learnt domestic science – dressmaking and cooking – took a Pitman's correspondence and typing course, and spoke French; in practice she learnt to ski. It wasn't enough to keep her there. After just six weeks she came home to London and refused to go back. Her mother was sympathetic, and so she embarked on a new life once more. This time, it was to be a life of independence.

THE BRIEF YEARS OF INDEPENDENCE

DIANA came back from Switzerland in March 1978, having had her fill. She spent her first few weeks in London, living in her mother's house, 69 Cadogan Place. The family was preparing for Jane's twenty-first birthday, to be followed by her wedding.

Jane, the sister with whom Diana had always got on best, and whom she is most like in temperament, had gone to Italy for six months after she left West Heath, to study art and history of art in Florence. Afterwards she took a secretarial course and joined the fashion magazine, *Vogue*, as an editorial assistant. Now, in April 1978, she was marrying Robert Fellowes, son of Sir William Fellowes, who used to be the Queen's land agent at Sandringham. Robert had lived on the estate for a while when he was a child, and was taught by Ally, the governess who had looked after the Spencer children. Robert was thirty-six when he married Jane, and a member of the Queen's permanent staff. He is now the Queen's assistant private secretary.

Diana was to be chief bridesmaid in a grand ceremony held in the Guards' Chapel, with a reception afterwards at St James's Palace, attended by the Queen Mother, the Duchess of Kent, Princess Alice, the Duke and Duchess of Gloucester, and, of course, all the family and staff from Althorp.

After the wedding, Jane and Robert moved into a grace and favour apartment at Kensington Palace, and they also have a house in the grounds at Althorp. Robert's job, however, tends to take him where the Queen is, and for the longer stays, for instance for the Queen's six weeks at Balmoral in the summer, Jane goes too. In June 1980 they had a baby, Laura, who provided good camouflage for Diana to spend some time at

Balmoral while Charles was there, without arousing suspicion from the press. These were precious weeks when Charles and Diana had a chance to get to know each other well enough, as the Prince was later to say, 'to realize there was something in it'.

After Jane's wedding, Diana began her first paid job in Hampshire, looking after Alexandra, the baby daughter of Major Jeremy Whitaker, a photographer, and his wife Philippa. Philippa Whitaker's younger brothers, the Straubenzees, had known the Spencer girls well – they used to shoot with them at Althorp. Diana went down to the Whitakers' home, quaintly named The Land of Nod, at Headley in Hampshire. She stayed with them for nearly three months, changing nappies, doing the washing, bathing the baby – doing whatever needed doing around the house, and living as one of the family.

In the summer she returned to London to her mother's house in Chelsea, which was to be her home for the next year. It was a big house on four floors, far too big for Diana on her own, and since Frances spent most of her time in Scotland, Diana invited Laura Greig, an old school friend from West Heath, to share with her. Laura spent her days at the Cordon Bleu cookery school, and Diana signed on with a couple of employment agencies and began to do temporary work. Knightsbridge Nannies provided babysitting jobs, while Solve Your Problems came up with anything – but as often as not cleaning work, which Diana loved.

During the summer Laura and Diana were joined in Cadogan Place by Sophie Kimball, who had stayed the course in Switzerland and done the full year. She is still one of Diana's closest friends, and it was through Sophie that Diana made many of the friends that she now has.

In July Diana celebrated her seventeenth birthday, which meant she was old enough to drive a car, and shortly afterwards enrolled at the British School of Motoring in Fulham Road. Driving wasn't second nature to her to begin with, although she had been driving on the roads at Althorp for some time, and the first time she took her test she failed it. She had applied to take it in Sevenoaks, for no better reason then that she had been at school there and knew the town quite well, but on the first occasion the examiner was of the opinion that knowledge of the town was not enough. Second time around she had an early morning test, after a late party the night before, and wasn't feeling her brightest. On this occasion, however, she could do no wrong for the examiner, and to everyone's surprise he passed her.

Even her loyalest friends have to admit that her driving was somewhat erratic in those days and they would get their seat belt fastened before they even closed the door. But in two years, by the time she was speeding away from telephoto lenses, she had improved beyond all measure.

Diana didn't have her own car immediately. She had the use of her mother's Renault 5, but most of the time travelled around London on a bicycle, and she continued to do that right up until the autumn of 1980. By that time her face was just too well known for it to be fun any more. But in 1978 no one would have given her a second glance.

With her two flat-mates, Laura and Sophie, and her two sisters, Diana had quite a pool of friends in London, and led a life that was never wildly extravagant or sophisticated, but was nevertheless very sociable.

She and her friends would spend the evening in one another's flats, maybe going out to have supper in a cheap bistro, and to a film, or maybe sitting at home with bowls of spaghetti bolognese, chatting and watching television.

Diana's friends were all from a similar background, ex-public school, most of them with parents living in the country. The girls, by and large, were artistic, had learnt to cook, and spent time travelling abroad; the boys were mostly old Etonians who joined the army, their family businesses, or went into the City. Alexandra Loyd, Diana's oldest friend from Norfolk, was living in London. So too were Caroline Harbord-Hammond and Mary-Ann Stewart-Richardson, who combined Norfolk with West Heath, and Theresa Mowbray, who was Frances's goddaughter and had also been at West Heath. Humphrey Butler was an old Etonian who used to shoot at Althorp and Rory Scott came into the picture via his sister Henrietta, who had shared a flat with Diana's sister

Jane. Simon Berry, of Berry Brothers, the wine merchants in St James's, was another old Etonian, like James Boughey who rose to favour in the group after scoring a half-century in the Eton-Harrow match in the summer of 1978. Yet another old Etonian friend was Harry Herbert, second son of the Queen's racing manager, Lord Porchester, and his younger sister Carolyn, who had been at school with Alexandra Loyd. And another childhood friend was Natalia Phillips, who in 1978 became the Duchess of Westminster. There were others, mostly old school friends, whom they occasionally saw, and there were periods when these friends went abroad for months at a time; but, despite this, the group remained more or less unchanged throughout Diana's years in London. Few people joined or fell from the ranks.

Most weekends they went to the country. Diana very seldom spent a Saturday or Sunday in London. Sometimes she went as one of a group to a house party or on her own to stay with friends. Occasionally she would go to Althorp to see her father, and usually she took a friend or two for company. More often than not they would stay in Jane and Robert's house on the estate.

In September Diana began a three-month cookery course with Elizabeth Russell at her small school in Wimbledon. She took the Underground out every morning from Sloane Square station and spent the day immersed in sponges, sauces and soufflés, some of which she would bring back home for everyone to eat that evening: all of them lived to tell the tale. She was actually a good cook and, when the course was over, made some money at it. She put her name down at Lumleys, yet another employment agency, which found her the occasional cocktail party for which to provide snacks. She even used to make and serve the canapés at her sisters' parties.

But those three months were a difficult time for Diana. In September, her father collapsed in the estate office in the stable block at Althorp with a cerebral haemorrhage and was taken into the house unconscious. Raine had been in London for the day and she came rushing home when she heard the news. Johnnie was soon taken to the local hospital, Northampton General, and then transferred to the National

Hospital in Queen Square in London, where for several months he lay in a coma. Almost everyone thought he would die. The family rallied round and drew closer than ever. But Raine became fiercely protective and in the interests of her husband wouldn't let anyone near Johnnie. She kept up a bedside vigil, holding his hand day in day out for the entire period he was in hospital. She literally willed him back to life, and whenever he talks about his illness now he says that without Raine he would be dead. Be this as it may, the fact remains that his four children went through a nightmare while he lay in a coma.

In November, just when he appeared to be recovering, Johnnie had a setback. An abcess that had formed on his lung burst. He was taken into intensive care once again, this time in the Brompton Chest Hospital, and again his life hung in the balance. Raine was no easy next-of-kin for the hospitals. If she thought her husband wasn't getting proper treatment she took him elsewhere. She also interfered with the drugs they were using. As she said in the interview with Jean Rook of the *Daily Express*, 'I'm a survivor, and people forget that at their peril. There's pure steel up my backbone. Nobody destroys me, and nobody was going to destroy Johnnie so long as I could sit by his bed – some of his family tried to stop me – and will my life force into him.'

James Whitaker, the most dedicated of all royal chroniclers, says that she gave instructions to the hospital staff at the Brompton to stop any of his children visiting him and disturbing him. As a result, Sarah, Jane and Diana would wait outside the back entrance of the hospital and, when Raine left via the front door, the nurses would sneak them up to their father when the coast was clear.

Raine's only response to the story, which appeared in *The Star*, was via her lawyer who said, 'Lady Spencer says the report is inaccurate but does not wish to comment further.' Her mother, Barbara Cartland, said of it: 'The children saw their father every day he was well enough to see anyone. There were three occasions when doctors allowed no one but his wife to see him because he was near to death.'

Friends of Diana's say that Raine did make it difficult for

them to see their father but, for all that, they do credit her for her devotion and bloody-minded determination during the four months of his illness.

In the end it was something more material than willpower that brought Johnnie Spencer round – it was a new drug. Raine is said to have heard of this drug which was available in Germany but not in Britain, and persuaded her friend Lord William Cavendish-Bentinck, now the Duke of Portland, who was then chairman of the British subsidiary of Bayer Chemicals, to get a supply. The drug did the trick. The fog on Johnnie's lungs began to clear, and when one day Raine played him excerpts from *Madame Butterfly* on a tape recorder, he opened his eyes and 'was back'.

He was finally released from hospital in January and went straight to the Dorchester Hotel in Park Lane to recover before eventually going home to Althorp in February. It had been an expensive recuperation. Johnnie and Raine were staying in a suite in the Dorchester costing £90 a night, and it was some weeks before he was fit enough to be taken home to Althorp. The total bill at the end of his illness was said to have been £60,000.

But although Johnnie made a miraculous recovery, those who know him well do notice that illness has slowed him down. His speech is slightly slurred, and he has a habit of repeating what people now say to him. He tires quickly and he has been forced to give up many of his activities in the county.

The very weekend Earl Spencer came out of hospital, Sarah and Diana were at Sandringham as guests of the Queen for a shooting party. Diana had never been a sentimentalist. She grew up in a household where shooting was as much of a weekend activity, season permitting, as washing the car. This doesn't detract from her love of animals in any way. Most people who shoot, or indeed hunt foxes, profess a great love of domestic animals and by and large treat their horses or their gun dogs with enormous kindness. They don't see that there is any contradiction in this and Diana has never had occasion to question the philosophy. In fact, she would be an odd one out in her social scene if she did.

That weekend in January 1979 was the beginning of Diana's

relationship with the Prince of Wales. It wasn't love at first. Diana still nurtured a schoolgirl crush on him, which she had had ever since their meeting in November 1977, and which he cannot have failed to notice and be flattered by. She wasn't very remarkable to look at in those days. Her hair was nondescript, shoulder length and much darker than today. She wore expensive but very conservative clothes, twin sets and tartan skirts, which would have suited her mother's generation far better. And she was agonizingly shy in unfamiliar territory.

But when she was among friends Diana Spencer was good company. She was no intellectual, but she could be relied upon to get everyone talking and laughing at dinner parties. She was fun and people liked to have her around. Charles probably didn't see his relationship with her as anything other than platonic in those days but he must have enjoyed her sense of humour and found quite refreshing her ease with him and her lack of sophistication. Whatever his feelings after that weekend at Sandringham, he began to see quite a lot of Diana. He would ring up Cadogan Place out of the blue and ask her out to the ballet or to the opera, often to make up numbers – she was always good value, and guaranteed to make everyone enjoy themselves. She wasn't a girlfriend – he had enough of those and enough trouble with those he had. She was simply someone with whom he felt he could relax and be himself.

Later that month, January 1979, Diana embarked on her last attempt at getting some qualifications. Her mother suggested that she should have a go at combining the two things she enjoyed most in life: dancing and children. And so she wrote to Miss Betty Vacani, the famous dancing teacher, who has been teaching offspring of the titled, rich and royal families to point their toes and skip and dance for the last fifty years or more.

Originally Betty Vacani ran the school with her aunt, the celebrated Marguerite Vacani, who is now dead, and her fifth floor studio in the Brompton Road is lined with photographs of the people that they taught from Princess Alice of Athlone down. Betty recalls Prince Charles as the very sweetest little boy she ever taught, and remembers teaching Diana's step-mother, Raine, to sharpen up her points when she was a child.

76

Diana already had a tenuous link with Miss Vacani. She had been taught at West Heath by a Vacani teacher and in an end-of-term competition one year, in which Diana had won a prize, Miss Vacani had been the judge. Diana, as she reminded Betty, had walked her pekinese dog round the grounds for her while she was at the school.

Miss Vacani actually had no memory of either Diana or the occasion at all, but is always prepared to help anyone who shows an enthusiasm for dancing. So she agreed to take Diana on as a student teacher for a fee of £100 a year.

By the time Diana began at the studio, the spring term had already begun. She cycled to the studio each morning in time for the babies' class when ten to twenty two-year-olds appeared on the floor in their dancing shoes, some boisterously, others nervously clutching nanny's or mummy's skirts and wanting to go home.

Diana's job was to scoop up the apprehensive tots by taking their hands and bringing them into the body of the class, and to calm the boisterous ones down, while 'Ring a Ring o' Roses' was played on the piano and everyone joined hands and danced. This would be followed by some toe-touching, hopping, and finally a round of 'Hickory Dickory Dock', the high spot of the morning's class. The children would all bring their own little toy for this from home, and when 'the mouse ran up the clock', they hid their mice away under their legs or inside their skirts, and brought them out again to everyone's great surprise when 'the clock struck one, and the mouse ran down. Hickory Dickory Dock'.

But love children as she did, Diana was out of her depth. Up till then she had only handled children on their own, or in twos at the most. She had never met twenty in one go before, and she was just too shy to cope, particularly with all the mothers and nannies sitting around the walls watching.

She was also in alien company, out of her 'safe' set. Betty Vacani was like everyone's favourite aunt and no one could ever have felt anxious with her, but the two other student teachers that year were glamorous and sophisticated, looking more as though they had come off the West End stage than out of a lap or 'Ring a Ring o' Roses'. While they would sit worrying about their weight, sipping Bovril through a straw at lunchtime, Diana would nip across the road to the Express Dairy in Montpelier Street and tuck into a good-sized chicken portion. She wasn't as sylph-like then as she is today.

Diana was an unworldly seventeen-year-old still, who wore no make-up and dressed in clothes her mother bought for her. But where other seventeen-year-olds might have tried to conform, to fit in with her fellow-students, Diana didn't. She never compromised; she left rather than try to become somebody that wasn't her. And this is what she has done now as Princess of Wales and probably why she will survive, where other people might have totally lost their identity. She has put on the smile and waves like a royal, but she dresses the way she wants to, has her hair done the way she likes and goes out and buys bubble gum if that's what she feels like doing. She will stride into the kitchens at Buckingham Palace to pinch a bit of cheese, just as she has done in her own homes all her life, and if it's not the done thing in royal households, that's tough.

Diana's days at the Vacani School didn't only involve babies. There were classes for older groups of children, too: the three-to-four-year-olds, the four-to-fives, the five-to-sevens, and the seven-to-nines, who by this time were on higher grades in the Cecchetti Method than Diana had ever taken at West Heath, and so she joined in the classes herself. She also took part in the mothers' ballet class.

She enjoyed the actual dancing very much, particularly the three classes in the week held for professional dancers. There was a two-hour Latin American class one morning, an advanced class taken by an ex-Diaghilev company dancer on another day, and a third class for no more than two or three people, taken by a Royal Ballet School soloist.

But although Diana was tremendously enthusiastic, and had a good natural turn-out of the feet, she wasn't good enough to have become a professional. If she had stuck with Betty Vacani it would have taken her three years, and three years of very hard work, to become a qualified classical ballet teacher. It would have taken her longer than most people, but then most of the pupils came to Betty Vacani with higher grades in the beginning.

But Diana didn't stay the course. She left before the end of term in March, never providing any proper explanation of why she was giving up. She simply didn't come any more, and when someone rang to see what had happened she explained that she had hurt her foot.

A few days later she went off skiing in the French Alps with a large party of friends, including Simon Berry, and surprised them all by her domesticity. With more than a dozen people living in one chalet, all out skiing every day, the place became a tip: dirty dishes were piled up in the kitchen sink, and odd items of clothing festooned the room like confetti.

When Diana injured her leg slightly she spent a day at home and cleaned the chalet from top to bottom. The sight of so much mess presumably hurt far more than the leg. She had been obsessively clean and tidy ever since she was a small child, and liked nothing better than to be let loose with a vacuum cleaner and a pile of dirty laundry. When she was at West Heath she had always done far more washing than any of the other girls, and on her weekends out, staying in her sisters' flats in London, she would also do their washing and the housework.

Now that she was living in London herself, this became a regular job. Once a week she would go and char for her sister Sarah at her flat for two hours, and now it was on a sound commercial basis.

The next couple of months after Diana came back from France were spent, in between other one-off cleaning and baby-sitting jobs, looking for a flat. On 1 July 1979 she turned eighteen, and came into money which had been left in trust for her. All the Spencer children had money in trust left by their American great-grandmother, Frances Work, to which they had access when they were eighteen. Their mother had encouraged them all to buy themselves a flat with the money, so that they could share with people of their own age. Sarah had bought a flat in Elm Park Lane, between the Fulham Road and the King's Road. Jane had bought hers in Warwick Square in Pimlico. And the flat Diana bought with her money was 60 Coleherne Court, said to have cost £50,000.

Sarah found her flat through her job at Savill's, the estate agents in Berkeley Square; her mother organized all the legal side of things for Diana, helped with the essential furnishings, and put her own builder on to the job of decorating; and Diana did the rest. It was a spacious flat in a four-storey mansion block on the corner of the Old Brompton Road, with high ceilings, fitted carpets and three bedrooms, which she and Sophie Kimball moved into in July. They were joined by a friend of Sophie's, Philippa Coaker, who had been at Eggleston Hall, a domestic science college in County Durham, with Sophie the year before she went to Switzerland.

Now that Diana had a flat of her own, Cadogan Place was too big and expensive to keep just for the occasional week in London, so Frances put the house on the market and took over Jane's flat in Warwick Square. Jane no longer used it after her marriage.

The flat in Coleherne Court was tastefully but traditionally furnished, with inoffensive colours and pretty wallpapers, and mostly comfortable modern furniture, bought from shops like Habitat.

Diana chose most of it herself, but never had the courage of her convictions. She would always bring samples back to the flat for the other two's approval before going ahead and buying anything she liked. But she enjoyed buying things for the flat; suddenly there was a whole new dimension to shopping.

Diana went up to Scotland that summer as usual to stay with her mother for a while and then with Jane in her cottage at Balmoral. When she came back to London she began a new job, helping at the Young England Kindergarten in St George's Square, Pimlico. She found the job through the old school network. It was run by Victoria Wilson and a West Heath old girl, Kay Seth-Smith, whose sister Janie had been a contemporary at the school with Diana's sister Jane. Jane had asked Janie if her sister might have a vacancy for Diana. By chance they had just started an afternoon group at the kindergarten for younger children on three afternoons a week and needed an assistant. Once again Diana fitted the bill and began work almost immediately.

The school wasn't much to look at and it was based in a large church hall, with a small stage, a slightly out-of-tune piano and swing doors through which the children crashed noisily both coming and going. They were privileged children – then paying £150 per term – and included Sir Winston Churchill's great-great-granddaughter, Harold Macmillan's great-grandson, and the son of the Agriculture Minister, Peter Walker.

Diana was known as Miss Diana, and away from the glare of mothers and nannies she was far more relaxed with the children than she had ever been at Miss Vacani's dancing studio. She cut up paper for them to paint on, helped them into their aprons, supervised them in the garden in St George's Square at playtime, sorted out their squabbles and took anyone on to her knee who was feeling a little tearful.

She was so good with the children that Kay and Vicky asked her to work in the mornings as well, when they had older children who went up to five. They had fifty children in all, and ten teachers, each teacher being in charge of a group of about five children.

Diana's main task was to organize their art work: to get out the glue pots and scissors, to recognize what the children had drawn, to mix the paints, and restrain any little Michelangelos who had designs on the walls. At the end of the morning she would help tidy the hall, wash up their coffee mugs, straighten chairs and pack away all the toys and equipment.

Diana was in her element. She had finally found something that she really enjoyed doing. When she was with her friends in the evenings she would chatter endlessly about the children. And as it became obvious to her that the children looked forward to seeing her in the mornings and were dependent upon her – if only to tie their apron strings – so she began to gain some confidence.

The Young England Kindergarten was a permanent job, but it wasn't full-time, which suited Diana down to the ground. Although she realized she could never dance professionally, she still loved it, and after ducking out of Vacani's in March, she had enrolled at the Dance Centre in Covent Garden. On her free afternoons she used to go up there to join the jazz and the tap classes, and sometimes the keep-fit sessions too.

She still did agency work when it came up, either cleaning or baby-sitting, and in the autumn undertook a job for Knightsbridge Nannies which lasted a whole year. She looked after a little American boy called Patrick Robinson, whose father was in the oil business. The family lived in Eaton Square, and Diana would take him over whenever she was asked, work at the kindergarten permitting, sometimes just for a morning, sometimes for the whole day. She adored Patrick; she would sit and play with him for hours, bring him back to the flat at Coleherne Court, or take him for long walks in his pushchair. If he fell asleep, she would sometimes shoot into Harrods and do her own shopping, still another of her favourite pastimes.

Her favourite shops in those days were Harrods and the other big Knightsbridge department store, Harvey Nichols. But, as the influence of her mother waned and that of her friends increased, she began to grow more adventurous in what she bought. She would go to shops like Fiorucci or Benetton for her clothes; although as often as not the clothes she actually wore weren't her own anyway. The girls in the flat all borrowed each other's things; their wardrobes were more or less communal.

There was a slight disruption in this happy routine that Christmas, when Philippa Coaker moved out of the flat to go abroad, and Virginia Pitman arrived. Virginia, like Philippa, was a friend of Sophie's from Eggleston Hall, and brought new life into Coleherne Court in the shape of a goldfish called Battersea. But in every other respect, life remained unchanged. Prince Charles continued to ring the flat every couple of months or so, although he never came to it. They would always arrange to meet at the ballet, or wherever they were going; as it was never a first night or special performance, no one ever took much notice. On other nights there might be dinner parties at home which were always guaranteed to be good with three trained cooks in residence, and if friends were coming who drank they brought their own bottles of wine.

Diana and her friends tended not to drink or smoke. They were clean-cut and wholesome – almost reactionary in their lifestyles. They had plenty of boyfriends and attracted more, but they were always chummy rather than flirtatious, and preferred to go out in a group rather than on individual dates.

On the occasions they ate out they never ate expensively, and the girls nearly always paid their own way. They would go to restaurants like the Poule au Pot in Ebury Street, the Santa Croce in Cheyne Walk, the San Quintino in Radnor Walk, or, one of Diana's favourites, Topolino D'Ischia in Draycott Avenue, for *tagliatelle* and a sing-along to Topolino's guitar.

On other evenings they might all dress up and go to the ballet. Diana's grandmother, Ruth, Lady Fermoy, used to arrange the tickets. Diana was close to her grandmother, and often used to go and see her in her flat in Eaton Square, sometimes taking little Patrick Robinson along too. It was always 'Granny' that Diana would turn to first if she was upset, in any sort of trouble, or worried about things. In some ways Ruth had taken over the role of mother, and Frances had become more of a friend.

At the beginning of 1980 there were more changes at Coleherne Court. Sophie had decided it was time for a change of scene and moved out. She was replaced by Carolyn Pride, who had known Diana at West Heath, although not very well; they had been in different work divisions and Carolyn had spent most of her time buried away in the music corridor. She had also been rather more successful in exams and had stayed on a year longer than Diana to take 'A' levels. She was now studying at the Royal College of Music, and in need of a bed and a home for her piano.

Another new addition was Ann Bolton, an ex-school friend of Alexandra Loyd, whom Diana had met on the ski slopes the year before. By coincidence Ann was working in the same office as Diana's sister at Savill's, and she had put them in touch again. Her appearance brought their total to four, and it was Virginia, Ann and Carolyn who became 'the flatmates' when the press discovered Diana that autumn.

Diana's flatmates always paid rent for their rooms, and they all paid their way with food and other communal things that they bought. The hallway was a constant jumble of bicycles and tennis racquets. Diana had a car, but she normally only used it when she went out to the country at the weekends. During the week she would use her bicycle with a basket on the front for her handbag and her shopping.

Not long after Diana had passed her driving test, Frances bought her a car of her own, first a Honda Civic, then a pale blue Volkswagen Polo, which she drove until she crashed it in 1980, coming out of a side-turning.

Her mother had always been very generous towards all of her children. Diana's father was careful by comparison, and his second wife had done nothing to change that. It was their mother who paid for Jane's and Sarah's weddings, and yet who had the grace, having paid, to let Raine take the front seat in the church.

When the Volkswagen had been put out of action, Frances bought Diana a bright red, brand-new Mini Metro, which was chased the length and breadth of England by journalists from every continent in the world throughout the winter of 1980; and which she frequently left as a decoy with a suitcase in the back seat, while she sped secretly away in someone else's car.

Despite the hallway, the inside of Coleherne Court was rather tidier than most shared flats because of Diana's preoccupation with neatness. She was always the first to get out the vacuum cleaner to clean the place up, and couldn't stand dirty plates in the kitchen. She never left the dishes until the morning, not even after a dinner party, and sometimes she would even start washing them before the party was over.

The flat was always full of life and noise. If Carolyn wasn't practising on the piano, the television would be on or there would be a record playing, usually something light by Neil Diamond, the Police or Abba. There were fashion magazines and copies of *Private Eye* on the coffee table in the sitting room and the mantlepiece was covered with invitations to parties.

But Diana didn't enjoy parties much. She went if she knew she was going to meet friends there, or if it was being given by a particular friend whom she liked very much, but she didn't go just for the sake of a party, and she had no interest in meeting new people. She hated nightclubs too, despite her passion for dancing; possibly because they were usually full of the sort of flamboyant, sophisticated people with whom she felt at her most insecure. She was happiest on home ground, surrounded by her friends.

She and her friends were almost interchangeable. They laughed at the same sort of jokes, enjoyed the same sort of films, read the same kind of books, wore the same kind of clothes, liked the same kind of music, and all had their hair cut by the same hairdresser, Kevin Shanley at Headlines in South Kensington, the man who created the 'Lady Diana haircut' that everyone copied, and who did her hair for the wedding.

Diana had been going to Kevin for years, ever since she had been living in London, and in recent years she has had her legs waxed and her eyelashes dyed at Headlines too. Even now Kevin cuts her hair but not always, as one might suppose, in the privacy of Diana's royal apartments. She still goes into Headlines from time to time, but very early in the morning when not many people are about: just one of the ways in which she is preserving her individuality and keeping in touch with the real world.

In the summer of 1980 Prince Charles had begun to take Diana seriously: she was seen in a party watching him play polo at Cowdray Park in July and dancing with him at the Goodwood Ball; she was on the royal yacht, *Britannia*, during Cowes Week; she then went up to Balmoral to stay with her sister Jane and to help look after her new baby; and in September she was spotted on her own with Charles, watching him salmon fishing on the banks of the River Dee.

The press put two and two together and on Monday, 8 September banner headlines proclaimed 'He's in Love Again' and named Diana as 'The New Girl for Charles'. That was effectively the end of her brief period of independence. She continued to live at Coleherne Court for the next five months, continued to work at the Young England Kindergarten, and continued to look after Patrick Robinson, but under an increasing shower of publicity. The flat was under siege day and night, and Diana had begun a trial by newspaper.

GETTING TO KNOW PRINCE CHARLES

NO ONE could ever seriously suggest that this romance was a case of love at first sight. Diana was a rather podgy baby when they first met; Charles an uneasy teenager just about to go off on yet another trial of misery to Gordonstoun. And, not surprisingly, neither remembers the first thing about it.

Their second meeting was more memorable. It was the weekend in November 1977 when Diana was still at West Heath and when Charles came to shoot on the Althorp estate as Sarah's boyfriend.

Prince Charles had arrived at the house on the Sunday afternoon in time for one of the famous Althorp Gala Dinners to which local Northamptonshire dignatories were invited. Thirty-two people sat down to dinner in the State Dining Room that evening around an enormous mahogany table laid with the finest silver and china. The Dining Room is one of the rooms on show to the public, added to the house by J. MacVicar Anderson in 1877 during the Red Earl's time. The walls are covered with crimson damask, taken from a Venetian palace, and hung with paintings of Diogenes and Cincinnatus by Salvatore Rosa that had been bought by the 1st Earl Spencer in 1764 on his grand tour of Italy.

For the Gala Dinner, the men wore dinner jackets and the women glittering ball gowns. Diana came down early from her room via the back staircase to show off her gown to the kitchen staff first. They remember remarking to one another how suddenly that night the schoolgirl they knew appeared to have become a young lady.

But although Charles and Diana technically sat down at the same table together, there were far too many people there that evening for them to meet. The Prince was, after all, the principal guest whom everyone had come for miles around to meet; and Diana was not much more than a child.

They met the next day, on the Monday morning during the shoot, and it was Sarah who introduced them. They had all converged in a ploughed field by Nobottle Wood, a beauty spot on the estate about two miles from the house.

Charles later said that his first impression of Diana had been, 'What a very jolly and amusing and attractive sixteen-year-old. I mean great fun – bouncy and full of life and everything.' Diana said she had thought Charles 'pretty amazing'; and Sarah subsequently said: 'They just clicked. He met Miss Right and she met Mr Right. I played Cupid.'

It seems likely that Sarah's account is a highly romanticized version, in which she has been wise after the event. At sixteen Diana was not the sort of girl that would have swept a twenty-eight-year-old man off his feet, particularly one who had some very beautiful women at his bidding. What does seem probable, however, is that this was where Diana fell for him. But she fell for him in the way that schoolgirls fall in love with pop singers or film stars: it was a crush.

Charles had all the magic of a pop singer or a film star and more; and although Diana had been brought up sharing cucumber sandwiches and a heated swimming pool with his younger brothers, the power and prestige of the monarchy had not entirely escaped her. Charles was probably the most famous man in Britain and certainly the most eligible bachelor. Diana could open a newspaper any morning of her school life to find a picture of Charles with some beautiful woman to whom the press was trying to marry him off, and in recent months one of these had been her sister.

Younger sisters have traditionally conceived passions for their big sister's boyfriends. Moreover, adolescent girls who spend nine months of the year shut away in all-girl boarding schools also traditionally fall for the first man that smiles at them on their weekends out. This is the stuff of which sixteen-year-old girls' dreams in boarding schools are made.

After the shoot that Monday morning the whole party went back to the stable block at Althorp for lunch: a steaming stew with mashed potatoes and Brussels sprouts, followed by one of the Prince of Wales' favourite puddings, treacle sponge. Soon after lunch Charles left and Diana went back to school for another month, to have a second go at her 'O' levels.

Diana was a romantic, and being in love with Prince Charles appealed to her romantic ideals, even if this was nothing more than a pipe dream. The sort of amateurish groping sessions that most girls of her age were busy indulging in with clumsy boys in the back row of the stalls offended those ideals. And Diana never had any wish to be part of them.

She had left school in December, a month after the first meeting with Charles, and after Christmas went away to Switzerland to the finishing school in the mountains. She was only sixteen and a half and young for her age, like many of the girls that came out of the shelter of West Heath. She had no qualifications, and no burning interests in anything except children and dancing. Her mother thought that six months or so away from home, mixing with girls from other countries in the safe environment of a school, speaking French, skiing and learning a few domestic skills would do her the world of good. But it didn't. Six weeks away from home was as much as Diana could take.

It can't have helped, as she was struggling with compulsory French and missing her family, to know that Charles and Sarah had gone to stay with the Duke and Duchess of Gloucester at Klosters and were whooping it up just over the mountain tops. So, once safely home in London for the Easter holidays, Diana broke the news to her parents that she wasn't going back.

The Prince was abroad when she returned to London, on a tour of South America, and the newspapers were filled with pictures of him lapping up the attentions of scantily clad Brazilian ladies.

Charles's relationship with Sarah had meanwhile come to an end. After their skiing holiday together, with the press doing a few calculations on the number of bedrooms per capita in the chalet, she had spoken out about their friendship and effectively killed stone dead any romance there might have been. In an interview with James Whitaker for *Woman's Own* she said:

He is a fabulous person, but I am not in love with him. He is a romantic who falls in love easily. But I can assure you that if there were to be any engagement between Prince Charles and myself it would have happened by now.

I am a whirlwind sort of lady as opposed to a person who goes in for long, slow-developing courtships. Of course, the Prince and I are great friends, but I was with him in Switzerland because of my skiing ability.

Our relationship is totally platonic. I do not believe that Prince Charles wants to marry yet. He has still not met the person he wants to marry. I think of him as the big brother I never had.

I wouldn't marry anyone I didn't love, whether it was the dustman or the King of England. If he asked me I would turn him down.

Her candour certainly put a stop to all the speculation, and the Prince of Wales took the knock to his macho image surprisingly well.

Sarah, the only red-haired member of the family, was the most extrovert of the sisters. As a child she once shocked her grandmother by bringing her pony into the house to introduce him to her. She enjoyed acting, was good at music and games, and misbehaved in her last year at school because she was bored. She is the only one who ever drinks – except for her brother Charles, who has grown into a very spirited young man himself – and she is the only one who has smoked cigarettes.

After an on-off engagement, Sarah was to marry Neil McCorquodale, an old Harrovian, ex-Coldstream Guards officer, in May 1980 in a relatively quiet ceremony at St Mary's Church, Great Brington, less than a mile from Althorp. She was twenty-five, he was twenty-eight, and coincidentally a relative of Sarah's stepmother, Raine. They now live near Grantham in Lincolnshire, where Neil farms his parents' estate.

Diana, meanwhile, settled down in London, spending her time doing temporary jobs. The next time that she and Prince Charles met was the very weekend her father came out of hospital, following his cerebral haemorrhage, in January 1979 when she and Sarah were invited to join a shooting party held by the Queen at Sandringham. Sarah had ended her romance with the Prince by talking to the press, but she hadn't ruined their friendship.

This weekend in Norfolk only served to confirm Diana's

feelings for Charles: she was still mad about him. But it gave him a chance to get to know her a little better. Charles found himself strangely attracted to her, though not in any consciously physical sense. She was still a fairly unprepossessing teenager – poles apart from the beauty that she was to grow into, while Charles was not short of beautiful women who attracted him in a physical sense.

He found Diana fun to be with and, of the friends he has made over the years, the majority have been people whom he has found entertaining. She wasn't intellectual in the slightest, but she did liven up the party. She wasn't quite as unpredictable as Sarah, but she was irreverently giggly and girlish, yet sensitive. In some ways she was a little girl, in other ways she showed uncanny maturity. It was a curious mixture, which Charles found appealing.

After that weekend Charles and Diana saw quite a lot of each other. He would ring her and invite her to join him for the evening – not specifically as his partner, but as one of a group. His romances were always so intense that it must have been quite a relief to be with someone he wasn't hopelessly in love with. She was an ideal companion: she laughed a lot, she was undemanding, she obviously liked to be with him which was flattering, she was young enough for no one to jump to any conclusions if they saw them together, and she was in many respects almost like one of the family.

If people were going to jump to conclusions, they would have paired Diana off with Prince Andrew, never Charles. Diana and Andrew in fact never had any kind of romance – they were chums, and not even very close chums. They sent each other Valentine cards occasionally as a joke, and, as Diana has said, they used to gang up with each other, but there was never any question of anything more than a kind of brother-sister relationship.

Diana didn't have much more than that kind of a relationship with anyone, although she had plenty of male admirers and would-be boyfriends. She simply wasn't interested. She would go out in a group with them, she was no killjoy and certainly no prude, but she never let anyone get close.

This may well have been because she was in love with Charles. It wasn't calculated; it wasn't because she knew that if she ever hoped to marry him she would have to be 'without a past'. It was pure romantic idealism, and if the man for whom she had conceived this passion had been the milkman's son next door, she would have felt the same way. She may also have felt slightly more wary of men than most girls of seventeen or eighteen because of her own parents' unhappy relationship. Whatever it was, admirers kept their distance.

Diana and Charles continued to meet periodically throughout 1979, sometimes every two months, sometimes there was longer between his calls. And that summer, soon after her eighteenth birthday, Diana went to stay with her sister Jane for a while at Balmoral, while the Royal Family was on holiday there.

During that year Diana had begun to become aware of herself and the way she looked. She had never been a girl who was looked at twice in the street; in fact when she was out of her own secure surroundings, she was so unassertive and undistinctive that people barely noticed whether she was there or not. If she came into a room she would hug the skirting board with her head firmly down, and only speak when spoken to.

People who had known her when she was seventeen couldn't believe that the Diana they were seeing in the news two years later was the same girl. She had moved into her own flat and chosen furnishings for it, she was driving her own car, and her job at the kindergarten was turning out to be a success. All this bolstered her very shaky ego, and with her new-found confidence she began to change her image, to assert herself. She cut her hair, put on some make-up from time to time, and chose clothes that reflected her own personality.

In February 1980 Diana was back at Sandringham again, in a house party organized by the Queen at Wood Farm, the house the Royal Family uses for short stays on the estate to save opening up the main house. She travelled up on the train to King's Lynn with Lady Amanda Knatchbull, Lord Mountbatten's granddaughter, and the girl that his favourite 'Uncle Dickie' had always hoped Charles would marry.

But Charles and Amanda were never anything more than very good friends. By this time Charles was in love again anyway with Anna Wallace. There had been a string of girls before her – Charles was a self-confessed romantic who admitted he fell in love very easily – and every time he did, of course, the newspapers were there to report his every sigh.

Anna Wallace was a little different from all the rest, and according to the people who made a study of such matters, this was the most passionate of all the Prince's romances. Anna was twenty-five years old, the daughter of a Scottish landowner, whom Charles had met out hunting with the Belvoir in November 1979. She had been private secretary to the fabulously rich Iranian socialite, Homayoun Mazandi, after Marie-Christine von Reibnitz had left the job to marry Prince Michael of Kent in June 1978.

Anna was known by her friends as 'Whiplash Wallace': she was fiery, wilful and unsuitable in every way. She admitted to having had previous lovers, as Nigel Dempster revealed in his column in the *Daily Mail*, the Queen disapproved of her, and so did Dale Tryon and Camilla Parker-Bowles, the two married women whose advice Charles normally took. But he was madly in love and, it is said, asked Anna to marry him.

Anna was stunned, but she turned him down. She knew she could never be accepted as the Prince of Wales's bride, nor could she accept the sacrifice of her freedom and independence for the trappings of royalty, to spend the rest of her life planting trees and shaking hands.

But Charles didn't end the relationship there. They continued to see each other, and in May 1980, three months after Diana had been at Sandringham, he took Anna on a secret holiday to Balmoral. At least it would have been secret had not the beady binoculars of the press been upon him, protected by the fact that there is no law of trespass in Scotland. He is said to have been angrier at the invasion of his privacy on this particular occasion than at almost any other time. He was clearly besotted with Anna.

The end came in the middle of June, over two days which began with the Queen Mother's eightieth birthday ball at Windsor Castle. The place was teeming with important guests with whom Charles felt obliged to spend some of his time – too much of his time, apparently. Anna was overheard to rage: 'Don't ever ignore me like that again. I've never been treated so badly in my life. No one treats me like that – not even you.'

But on the next public occasion he treated her in exactly the same way and that was his mistake. It was at Stowell Park in Gloucestershire, where Lord Vestey was throwing a polo ball, and Charles ostentatiously had one dance after another with Camilla Parker-Bowles. He didn't even pause long enough to invite his hostess to dance.

Anna was furious and halfway through the evening borrowed Lady Vestey's car and drove back to London, never to be seen with the Prince again. It is said that the Prince was shattered and did everything in his power to persuade Anna to let him explain, but she refused. That same month she became engaged to and then married another man, the Honourable John Hesketh.

That summer Diana went up to Balmoral to see her sister Jane and her new baby and found Charles there, nursing his battered pride and broken heart. Being dumped by Anna had been a sobering experience. He had been living the life of the great Casanova for so many years with women falling over themselves to please him. After all, who was going to say no to the man who will one day be King of England? It took Anna Wallace to bring him down to earth, and the experience hurt, but it also made him think long and hard about what he was doing with his life.

Diana was there as a friend to turn to at a very necessary moment. She was as soft, cheerful and bouncy as ever, still dancing attendance, still hanging on his every word, enjoying his company, boosting his ego, and still waiting for some show of affection from him, like a puppy underfoot. And, as the weeks went past, Charles gradually began to notice her, to notice that she was no longer a 'very jolly and amusing and attractive sixteen-year-old', but that she was a fully-grown nineteen-year-old whom he enjoyed being with, who was fun, and who was clearly in love with him.

By this time the pressure on Charles to marry and produce an heir had become intense, not just from his parents, who thought it was high time he settled down, and the press, who thrived on the speculation and had been marrying him off since the age of three, but from the British public too.

Apart, ironically, from Charles's great-uncle, the Duke of Windsor, who had given up his throne to be with the woman he loved, and who was nearly forty when he married Mrs Simpson, the last Prince of Wales to have reached thirty without being married was James Stuart, the Old Pretender, and even he had married the following year, in 1719. Charles's own father had married at twenty-six, when his mother was twenty-one. His grandfather, George VI, had married at twenty-seven; his great-grandfather, George V, at twenty-eight; and his great-great-grandfather, Edward VII, had married when he was twenty-one.

Charles himself had indicated in an interview when he was twenty-seven that he thought thirty 'about the right age for a chap like me to get married'. And when his thirtieth birthday came and went, and with it no let up in the stream of suitable and unsuitable girls that dangled from his arm, the press and the public grew ever more impatient. Charles must have been well aware that time was running out, not to mention suitable candidates. He spoke of it often; but he was also aware that falling in love and finding someone to marry were not necessarily connected and he was going to have his share of love affairs while he might.

He had once said:

Whatever your place in life, when you marry you are forming a partnership which you hope will last for fifty years. So I'd want to marry someone whose interests I could share. A woman not only marries a man; she marries into a way of life – a job. She's got to have some knowledge of it, some sense of it; otherwise she wouldn't have a clue about whether she's going to like it. If I'm deciding on whom I want to live with for fifty years – well, that's the last decision on which I want my head to be ruled by my heart.

On another occasion he said:

I think an awful lot of people have got the wrong idea of what it is all about. It is rather more than just falling madly in love with somebody and having a love affair for the rest of your married life. Much more than that. It's basically a very strong friendship . . . I think you are very lucky if you find the person attractive in the physical *and* the mental sense. . . . To me marriage seems to be the biggest and most responsible step to be taken in one's life.

The same might be said for any man contemplating marriage, but Charles of course had further complications to consider, which he obviously did consider carefully. In another interview he observed: 'When you marry in my position you are going to marry someone who perhaps one day is going to be Queen. You have to choose somebody very carefully, I think, who could fill this particular role. . . . The one advantage about marrying a princess, for instance, or somebody from a royal family, is that they do know what happens.'

'The only trouble,' he added, 'is that I often feel I would like to marry somebody English. Or perhaps Welsh. [It was just a few days before his investiture as Prince of Wales.] Well, British, anyway.'

Suitable and available princesses were very thin on the ground, and British princesses non-existent. The next best thing was the aristocracy, and Diana belonged to one of the most noble families in Britain, and actually had more English royal blood in her veins than the Prince of Wales himself.

She also had as good an idea of what the 'way of life – the job' was about as any non-royal could have. Her two grandmothers had been in service to the Queen Mother, and her father had been in service to the Queen. The families had also been friends for generations, and Diana was as much at ease with his family as she was with any other.

His final qualification was that anyone he chose as a wife should first and foremost be a friend. 'Essentially you must be good friends,' he had reiterated, 'and love, I am sure, will grow out of that friendship.' And Diana was undoubtedly a friend. The fact that he wasn't 'in love' with her was not of paramount importance.

There was one further qualification which had been left unsaid in all his utterances on the subject of marriage, but which, as past events had proved, was on the list nevertheless. His bride would need to be pure as the driven snow. Whatever his own feelings about marrying a virgin may have been, he couldn't run the risk of any ex-lover stepping forward to make his fortune by selling the story of his torrid nights of love with the future Queen of England to the Sunday newspapers. It was his duty to present his public with perfection.

And so that summer Charles began to take his responsibilities seriously, and as Diana later said, she happened to be in the right place at the right time. She also happened to be perfect for the job. She fulfilled all the qualifications and, better still, she wasn't hell-bent on a career, as at least one of the previous girls Charles must have considered – Lady Jane Wellesley, the Duke of Wellington's daughter – had been. The career Diana had mapped out for herself was marriage and children, and Charles could hardly be accused of interfering with that. During the July of 1980 the seeds were sown in his mind but it was not something he was going to rush. He also had to be careful how he wooed Diana. She was young and shy, and the publicity that would be bound to follow any public display of courtship might well, he feared, have frightened her off; it had others.

That month he invited her to watch him play polo with Les Diables Bleus at Cowdray Park in Sussex, along with several other guests, and to the ball at Goodwood House afterwards, where they danced together. Then, in the first week of August, he asked her to join a party on board the royal yacht, *Britannia*, moored off the Isle of Wight for Cowes Week. Prince Andrew and Prince Edward were on board too, together with their cousins James and Marina Ogilvy. It was predominantly a young party and they all had a lot of fun. Diana enjoyed herself, particularly the day she flicked the mast of Charles's windsurfer and sent him flying over backwards into the chilly Solent. But for all the fun and games, Diana was said to have been dejected that week because Charles didn't seem to be paying her enough attention.

He soon remedied that. After her arrival back in London, two dozen dark red roses were left outside her door at Coleherne Court one afternoon; shortly to be followed by an invitation to Balmoral. Once again she wasn't the only guest, but this time Charles did pay her some attention. Unfortunately, so did the press. The same pair of binoculars that had homed in on Charles with Anna Wallace on the banks of the River Dee just four months previously spied a new mystery girl in his life, and the search was on for her identity.

The neck around which this particular pair of binoculars hung belonged to one of the most shameless and dedicated 'Charles Watchers' in Fleet Street, James Whitaker, who writes principally for the *Daily Star*. For the last seven years he has done nothing but chase Charles, document his life, scrutinize his girlfriends, and spy on him round the clock. He had been highly critical of some of Charles's previous conquests, and quite graphic in the intimate description of his relationships with others, but Diana had his full approval. He is possibly as besotted with Diana as Charles will ever be, and his affection grew from the very first day he spotted her, because for the first time in seven years he had found someone who was as cunning as he was.

Diana was standing on the banks of the river watching Charles fish. But she only had one eye on Charles. The other was watching Mr Whitaker, as she came to call him, and his photographer through a small hand mirror, which meant it was impossible for them, even if they spotted her, to get a look at her face.

When they tried to flush her out of her hiding place behind a tree she turned with enormous cool and walked straight up a one-in-two hill without turning her head once. As she was wrapped up in a headscarf and flat cap, they hadn't a clue to her identity.

However, it didn't take Mr Whitaker and his colleague long to find out, or indeed to discover where Diana lived in London. From that day forward until the day she became engaged five months later, there were newspapermen camped on the doorstep round the clock, ready to follow her every move.

In the early days she paid very little attention to them. She was polite when they greeted her, blushed if they asked if she was in love with Charles, and when pressed said things like:

'You know I cannot talk about my feelings for him.' But for the most part, she carried on with her life as though nothing had happened. She still went to the Young England Kindergarten in the mornings, still went shopping in the supermarket round the corner and still took out Patrick Robinson, the little boy she baby-sat for, in his pushchair. The only difference the press had made to her life was that she had to give up her bicycle and go everywhere by car.

On one occasion she even went out of her way to oblige the gentlemen of the press, an occasion which she will probably be teased about for the rest of her life. She agreed to pose for photographers in the gardens at St George's Square with a couple of the children from the kindergarten, on condition that they would then leave her alone and stop disrupting her work with the children.

What she didn't realize, and what the photographers were in no hurry to point out to her, was that when she stood with the light behind her, her skirt was entirely see-through. The result was some memorable pictures which appeared first in the London *Evening Standard* and thereafter in just about every newspaper and magazine in the world. Diana was horrified. Charles is said to have been amused. 'I knew your legs were good,' he is reported to have told her, 'But I didn't realize they were that spectacular. And did you really have to show them to everybody?'

Charles could afford to be amused – he was used to it. If he hadn't had a sense of humour about the outlandish stories that newspapers have printed about him over the years, or the embarrassing photographs that have highlighted his every nose-pick, he would have gone mad. But Diana was new to it, and the skirt episode was only the first of several that reduced her to tears.

As time passed Diana grew constantly less naïve with the press. Although still impeccably behaved towards them, she learned a little cunning and succeeded in outwitting them on a number of occasions. For instance, she and Charles spent some time together in October staying with the Queen Mother at Birkhall, her home on Deeside in Scotland. No one ever knew about this until Charles and Diana admitted they had been there in the interviews they gave at the time of their engagement.

Their next public appearance together, if not exactly side by side or arm in arm, was at Ludlow in Shropshire on 24 October, where Diana had driven from London to watch Charles race his horse Allibar over jumps in the Clun Handicap Race for amateur riders. Having put money on him she sat and watched the race, squealing with excitement as he came over the last fence; she was with his trainer's wife, Judy Gaselee, and Camilla Parker-Bowles. Camilla and Dale Tryon, known as Kanga, may not have approved of Anna Wallace, but Diana had their blessing – she was halfway home.

After the race meeting at Ludlow Diana and Charles went to spend the weekend with the Parker-Bowles at their house in Wiltshire. On the following day Charles and Andrew Parker-Bowles went cubbing with the Beaufort Hunt, while Camilla and Diana spent the morning together. On the Sunday Charles drove Diana over to Highgrove in Gloucestershire, to show her the house that he had bought.

The following weekend they were back, staying with the Parker-Bowles for the first meet of the season. Diana again stayed at home with Camilla, while Charles went off with Andrew to join the hunt shortly after they had moved off so as not to disrupt the meet itself.

A couple of days later they were together again at the Ritz Hotel in London, at Princess Margaret's fiftieth birthday party on 4 November. The next day Charles went off on an official visit to the West Country and spent the night of 5 November on the royal train in a siding at Holt in Wiltshire. That night, according to a story which subsequently appeared splashed all over the front page of the *Sunday Mirror*, Diana drove from London for a secret rendezvous with Charles aboard the train; it was dubbed 'Love in the Sidings', and Diana was said to have been allowed to drive through the police checkpoint to the deserted sidings, and was then escorted by a detective on to the train. Some hours later she had emerged, according to the story, walked back to her car, and driven home to London.

The following night, the press claimed, she had arranged a similar exercise: she had driven up from London earlier, stayed at a house belonging to a close friend of Charles's, and gone to the train, again in the middle of the night, while the police had kept guard in a chicken farm.

When the story appeared on 16 November, two days after Charles's thirty-second birthday, Diana was once again devastated. She was particularly shocked that a newspaper should print such lies about her when they had rung her up before printing the story to ask if it was true, and she had told them it wasn't. 'Afterwards they rang up to apologize, but that doesn't change people's minds about what they think when they read a story like that,' she later said. 'The trouble is people believe what they read.'

Prince Charles and the Queen were both furious, uncharacteristically so, in defence of Diana's reputation, and the Queen took the unprecedented step of instructing her press secretary, Michael Shea, to demand a retraction. She and the rest of the Royal Family had taken to Diana whole-heartedly and were hopeful that the interest Charles was showing in her might come to something. They didn't want anything to scotch its chances.

The editor of the *Sunday Mirror*, Bob Edwards, refused to retract on the basis that he believed the original report had been true in all essential matters, and he was satisfied that it in no way reflected badly on Prince Charles or Lady Diana. Instead he printed an exchange of letters with the Palace.

As he explained to me later, no couple are actually going to make love on a train surrounded by at least half of the Wiltshire police force. The story simply proved that she was so much in love with him that she would drive a hundred miles through the night just to be with him for a couple of hours – and *not* make love!

The Sunday on which the exchange of letters appeared, Charles left for an official tour of India and Nepal, while Diana was left to counter the allegations on her own, which she did. She insisted that she had never been on the royal train and didn't even know what it looked like but that she'd spent the night in question in her flat with her flatmates and, exhausted after her late night at the Ritz, had gone to bed early.

The next day a story appeared on the leader page of the *Daily Mail* written by Danae Brook, who lived in the same block of flats as Diana, and to whom Diana had talked frankly in the belief that she was nothing more than a kindly neighbour. Diana was upset, but things came to a head a couple of days later when the Press Association put out a report in which Diana was reputed to have said: 'I'd like to marry soon.'

In the early days Diana had found all the attention quite a joke, but now it was becoming too much for her, and she began to feel panicky. There were hordes of reporters and photographers camped in the street outside Coleherne Court, keeping a round-the-clock vigil. Journalists rang her at all hours, often in the middle of the night or in the small hours of the morning. Every time she went out she was followed. Everyone she spoke to turned out to be from the press. Every time she spoke to the press knowingly, they ignored what she had said and wrote what they would have liked her to say. For a period Diana became quite frightened. She wasn't used to all this attention; in fact it is probably true to say that no one, certainly no one connected with the Royal Family, has ever had the kind of attention that has been paid to Diana, either before or after the engagement and even the wedding. Diana had an effect on the press and the British public that no one could ever have foreseen.

At the beginning of December Diana's mother, Frances Shand Kydd, wrote to *The Times* in her daughter's defence, as she said later, entirely off her own bat, without consulting anyone:

In recent weeks many articles have been labelled 'exclusive quotes', when the plain truth is that my daughter has not spoken the words attributed to her. Fanciful speculation, if it is in good taste, is one thing, but this can be embarrassing. Lies are quite another matter, and by their very nature, hurtful and inexcusable. . . .

May I ask the editors of Fleet Street, whether, in the execution of their jobs, they consider it necessary or fair to harass my daughter daily, from dawn until well after dusk? Is it fair to ask any human being, regardless of circumstances, to be treated in this way? The freedom of the press was granted by law, by public demand, for very good reasons. But when these privileges are abused, can the press command any respect, or expect to be shown any respect?

Mrs Shand Kydd was clearly wondering, and was not alone in wondering, just how much more Diana was going to be able to stand. Sixty MPs tabled a motion in the House of Commons 'deploring the manner in which Lady Diana Spencer is treated by the media' and 'calling upon those responsible to have more concern for individual privacy'. Fleet Street editors met senior Press Council members to discuss the matter. It was the first time in the twenty-seven-year history of the Press Council that such an extraordinary meeting had been convened. But still the 'harassment' continued, virtually unabated.

When Prince Charles arrived back from India in December, Diana was hounded from pillar to post so that the popular papers wouldn't miss the story of their reunion. She was even driven to fleeing out of the fire exit of a Knightsbridge store on one occasion and climbing over dustbins to try to get away from reporters. And guess how we know that?

But Diana was just as determined as they were, and not without a few tricks of her own. She packed up her car as though going away for the weekend, with a suitcase, a coat and a pair of wellington boots, then locked it up and walked away, pretending to buy something from the shops round the corner. By the time she returned she had been further than the shops. She had again been up to the Queen Mother's home in Scotland, Birkhall, where she and Charles spent a happy weekend together, while the press twiddled their thumbs in the Old Brompton Road and realized they'd been 'had'.

The Queen Mother was a willing accomplice. There are many people who believe that the match was contrived by her with the connivance of Diana's grandmother, Ruth, Lady Fermoy, the Queen Mother's Lady-in-Waiting, who has always been ambitious for her family to marry well. The occasional word of encouragement dropped into Diana's ear during those years of unrequited passion may well have helped to keep her true. And it would have been quite natural for the Queen Mother to try to do a little match-making for her favourite grandson. They must have sat and discussed his problems in finding a suitable bride on innumerable occasions over the years. The Queen Mother is certainly not on record as ever having offered Birkhall before as a secret meeting place for Charles and any of his other girlfriends. There is no question that Diana had her full approval from the start.

Charles and Diana spent Christmas and the New Year apart. Diana was at Althorp, while Charles was at Windsor and then Sandringham, and for once the Royal Family had some inkling of just what 'harassment' Diana had been going through. They couldn't move without being photographed or followed, and they handled it with rather less good humour than Diana. The Queen bellowed 'Why don't you go away?' in a most unregal tone of voice, someone fired a shotgun over the head of a photographer from twenty yards away, and Prince Charles came over to a group of journalists and said: 'I should like to take this opportunity to wish you all a very happy New Year and your editors a particularly nasty one.'

The situation had been badly handled all round. The press were simply interested in whether Diana was at Sandringham and since no one would issue a statement one way or the other, they maintained their vigil. They may not have had a right to know, but they certainly had a readership who wanted to know.

Diana, having spent Christmas at Althorp, saw the New Year in in London with friends, and drove up to Sandringham the following day. The next time she and Charles met was a week later at Highgrove, which, again thanks to cunning subterfuge and the assistance of friends who acted as decoys, she reached without her chaperones from the press. The following morning, however, they caught up with her. She had gone up to the Berkshire Downs at the crack of dawn to watch Charles exercise Allibar. But the relentless Mr Whitaker was there, having spotted her car parked outside Charles's trainer's house in Lambourn.

Charles can't have failed to be impressed by the way Diana handled the press. If it had been part of the suitability test, she would have come through heroically. She always called the regulars that she recognized by their names and always said 'Good morning' politely. The only time that she ever asked them to leave her alone was because the children in the kindergarten were being upset and frightened by the photographers' flash guns.

103

There was just one more meeting that became public. That was a day at Sandringham, before Charles went off skiing for two weeks in Klosters with friends. He returned from Switzerland on 3 February, and saw Diana briefly. Two days later they had dinner together in his apartments at Buckingham Palace and, after dinner that night, as Charles later admitted on his engagement day, he had asked Diana to marry him.

She went back to Coleherne Court that night and the next morning broke the news to all her flatmates, who were thrilled to bits. But her friends from the press had to wait three more weeks before the engagement was announced officially. In the meantime, Diana had her first break in five months and her last holiday as an ordinary member of the public.

THE ENGAGEMENT

PRINCE CHARLES had first raised the subject of marriage with Diana in the inauspicious surroundings of the Parker-Bowles' cabbage patch. This meeting took place before Christmas in 1980, just one of the many during their courtship of which the press and public were unaware. It was not so much a proposal, as a probing, 'If I were to ask, what do you think you might answer?' to which Diana is said to have just giggled. There was no question, even then, what her reply would have been.

When he finally did ask the question proper in February, Charles had suggested to Diana that she shouldn't answer immediately, but should reflect on it while she was away in Australia, 'to think if it was all going to be too awful'. Again there was nothing for Diana to think about. She had made up her mind a long time before that she wanted to marry Charles – she hadn't been through five months of hell for nothing. She would have had more to think about if he hadn't asked her to marry him.

She was young, she was idealistic, and in love for the very first time. Marriage and children were all that mattered, and as long as she had those, nothing could be 'too awful', any way of life would be good. She knew there would be millions of hands to shake, tedious ceremonies and speeches scheduled for her week after week, but even those seemed exciting in the abstract. And Charles would be with her.

In Charles, Diana saw a chance to belong; to belong to someone whom she could love and give herself to completely and utterly without the fear that he would leave her. At the age of six she had been hurt badly when her mother had left home, and she had been wary of trusting anyone wholeheartedly ever since.

Charles was someone she could trust. He was almost the one and only person in the land for whom marriage had to be permanent. As he had said himself six years previously, in stressing the importance of finding the right woman,

In my position, obviously, the last thing I could possibly entertain is getting divorced.

Marriage is a much more important business than falling in love, as I think a lot of couples probably find out. It is not just for the sake of living with a girl but more a question of creating a secure family unit in which to bring up children and give them a happy, secure upbringing – that's what marriage is all about . . . I hope I will be as lucky as my parents, who have been so happy.

All this was music to Diana's ears. And when she did become engaged to Charles, she told friends that for the first time in her life she had felt secure.

But this seriousness was an undercurrent. Diana's immediate reaction to Charles's proposal was pure unadulterated excitement. She could hardly contain it. Her sister Sarah said afterwards that Diana hadn't told her she was engaged, she had seen it all over her face. 'I saw Diana in her London flat,' she said, 'and I guessed when I saw her face. She was totally radiant, bouncing, bubbling and I said, "You're engaged," and she said, "Yes".'

But they all had to keep the news to themselves for three more weeks, because the very night after Charles had proposed at Buckingham Palace, Diana flew to Australia with her mother and step-father for a holiday which they were all determined should be secret. The three of them left Heathrow Airport on a scheduled Qantas flight to Sydney, and no one but the captain had any idea that Diana was on the plane. From Sydney they drove to the Shand Kydd's sheep-station at Yass, which bordered a vast property owned by Rupert Murdoch, and thus for a day and a half they sat right under the nose of one of the most powerful newspaper magnates in the world who, in addition to his Australian and American papers, owns the *News of the World*, the *Sun* and *The Times*.

The British press had lost her, and when they rang Mrs Shand Kydd to ask if Diana was with her, Frances denied it. It was the first and last downright lie anyone told in the entire saga, but it had the desired effect. The Australian press, however, were not so gentlemanly. They didn't telephone, they arrived in a helicopter which they had chartered from a local television station. They circled the property a few times and then landed right beside the house, and reporters and photographers were suddenly everywhere.

At this juncture some close friends came to the rescue and Peter Shand Kydd indulged in some *Boy's Own* skulduggery which he enjoyed enormously: speeding across the countryside, unscrewing car number plates, sending out decoys, and finally losing their 'tail'.

For ten days they enjoyed total peace and quiet in a friend's beach house on the coast of New South Wales; Diana swam and surfed and caught up on a lot of lost sleep, while a ring of trusted friends kept invaders at bay. Even Charles had trouble getting through. 'I rang up on one occasion and I said: "Can I speak?"' he recounted in a television interview later. 'And they said: "No, we're not taking any calls." So I said: "It's the Prince of Wales speaking." "How do I know it's the Prince of Wales?" came back the reply. I said: "You don't. But I am," in a rage. And eventually . . . I mean, I got the number because they were staying somewhere else. They said the phones were tapped or something – which I found highly unlikely. . . . '

Peter Shand Kydd was triumphant that it had worked so well, and Frances remained quite unrepentant on their return when she finally admitted she had lied to the press. 'I was determined to have what my daughter and I both knew to be our last holiday together,' she said. The Shand Kydds didn't return until the day after the engagement had been announced. Diana had left ahead of them, travelling *incognito* once again, and was so successful in her subterfuge that she was back in London for two full days before she was discovered by the press.

Charles was at Highgrove busy training for the Cavalry Hunters Chase at Chepstow, in which he planned to race his horse Allibar on the Saturday afternoon. After a couple of days in London, Diana drove up to join him. Next morning they were both up at the crack of dawn for Charles to ride out from his trainer's stables in Lambourn along the Mandown Gallops on the Downs, while Diana watched. Allibar was going well. He had done his seven furlongs, and Charles was walking him quietly home for breakfast when the eleven-year-old horse suddenly shuddered, staggered and collapsed to the ground with a massive heart attack.

Charles leapt to the ground as soon as he realized something was wrong, and cradled the dying horse's head in his arms. Diana came running across to help, but there was nothing anyone could have done. Even so Charles refused to leave his horse until the vet had arrived and certified that Allibar was really dead.

But the busy schedule of royalty doesn't cater for personal grief. Charles had to be in Swansea that afternoon to be given the Freedom of the City, and look pleased about it for the hundreds of people who had turned out in the freezing cold to see him. Meanwhile Diana went back to London. But tragic though the morning had been, sharing it had probably brought Charles and Diana even closer together.

The next day Charles rang Earl Spencer at his London flat in Grosvenor Square and formally asked for Diana's hand in marriage. 'Can I marry your daughter?' he said, simply. 'I have asked her and very surprisingly she has said yes.' To which Diana's father replied, 'I'm delighted. Well done,' adding, when speaking about it later, 'I don't know what he would have done if I'd turned him down.'

The Queen, not surprisingly, had been in on the Prince's intentions for some time. Quite apart from a natural desire to have his mother's approval, as heir to the throne he was going to need it officially under the Royal Marriages Act of 1772, introduced in the reign of George III. But there had never been any doubt that he had the Queen's approval. The Queen is not a woman who takes to everyone, and she makes no bones about those people she doesn't take to, but she had liked Diana from the start. All the Royal Family had liked her, and they had all been immensely impressed by the way she had stood up to the publicity that she had experienced over the previous five months. She was relaxed with them, charming, pretty, and fun – enjoying all the silly party games they played at Christmas – and, best of all, appeared to be having a very good effect on Charles. He seemed more relaxed than he'd been for a long time.

That Saturday night the Queen threw a big family dinner party at Windsor for Charles and Diana to celebrate, and the next day Charles gave Diana her ring. On Monday the Prime Minister, Margaret Thatcher, and the Leader of the Opposition, Michael Foot, were told the news, and Mrs Thatcher passed it on to members of the Cabinet. Coded telegrams were sent out to Commonwealth heads of state, to the heads of other governments and to the Archbishop of Canterbury. The Spencer family spent the day passing on the news, in strictest confidence of course, to close members of the family and godparents, and that evening Lord Spencer rang trusted members of the staff at Althorp to tell them too.

All that remained was to let the nation in on the secret, and Charles was passionate that the Palace should beat Fleet Street to it. He failed. The front page of *The Times* on Tuesday morning, 24 February, carried the simple heading, 'Engagement of the Prince to be announced today.'

Someone in the know had leaked the story to William Rees-Mogg, at that time the editor of *The Times*. Although the finger has been pointed at various people since, no one but he knows who it was for sure, and he's not telling.

Whoever it was, the information was absolutely right. At 11 a.m. the Queen's Press Secretary, Michael Shea, issued an announcement to the Press Association. The Queen was about to begin an investiture at Buckingham Palace, and at 11 o'clock precisely the Lord Chamberlain, Lord Maclean, stepped forward and addressed the 150 people who had come to receive honours and awards. 'The Queen has asked me to let you know,' he said, 'that an announcement is being made at this moment in the following terms: "It is with the greatest pleasure that The Queen and The Duke of Edinburgh announce the betrothal of their beloved son, The Prince of Wales, to The Lady Diana Spencer, daughter of The Earl Spencer and The Honourable Mrs Shand Kydd".'

At long last months of speculation were at an end. Gone, in a fifteen-second statement, was one of Fleet Street's longest running stories; for twenty-nine years, any thoughts, however far-fetched, on whom Charles might marry were worth a few column inches.

Everyone was delighted: people in the streets greeted one another with the news; share prices on the London Stock Market rose; Prince Charles's old minesweeper, HMS *Bronington*, fired a twenty-one-gun salute in Portsmouth harbour in honour of its former skipper and his bride; letters and telegrams began to pour into Buckingham Palace, and there were loud cheers in both Houses of Parliament.

The only sour note came from Willie Hamilton, Labour MP for Fife Central, a vociferous anti-monarchist, who was on his honour to say something, and was given the perfect opportunity by the latest unemployment figures which coincidentally were published on the same day.

During the next few months we shall have further distractions from the results of the Government's disastrous policies as the celebrations get under way. There will be no question of cash limits [for the wedding], a six per cent restriction, or worry about the impact on the public sector borrowing requirement. The sky will be the limit. And the British people, deferential as always, will wallow in it. The winter of discontent is now being replaced by the winter of phoney romance.

Willie Hamilton couldn't have been more wrong. We were in 'for six months of mush' as he predicted, and the sky very nearly was the limit, but the British people were far from deferential. They willed it and they wallowed in it, and if they had been asked to go without their summer holidays for it, they probably would have done that too. The British people were transported out of their own winter of discontent into a fairytale. And if Diana herself had spoken from the balcony at Buckingham Palace and announced that she was only marrying the Prince for his money, no one would have believed her.

Of course she wasn't about to declare anything of the sort, and her first opportunity to say anything at all was in the very same room, Charles's private sitting room at Buckingham Palace, where he had proposed to her three weeks earlier.

Michael Shea had been called home from a family holiday in

Norway to handle the announcement and the interviews with the press that followed. The only two journalists that he had invited in the morning were the Court correspondents of the Press Association, through which the official announcement had been made, and of BBC radio: Grania Forbes and David McNeil.

To get things going, both journalists were presented with half a dozen questions for them to ask which Michael Shea, Charles and Diana had hatched amongst them beforehand. They were allowed to add questions of their own, but the Prince had to be shown them and agree to them first. But it was Diana's first real interview ever, and probably the most personal Charles has ever given, so they were naturally nervous.

The questions concerned where Diana and Charles had first met, when Charles had proposed, where they planned to spend their honeymoon, the date of the wedding, and where they would live after they were married. One question that Grania Forbes added to the list was whether they were bothered by the age-gap between them, to which Diana replied that she hadn't really thought about it, and Charles said, 'It's only twelve years. Lots of people have got married with that sort of age difference. I just feel you're as old as you think you are . . . Diana will certainly help keep me young . . . I think I shall be exhausted!'

Charles considered that Diana would make an ideal Princess of Wales, 'I'm sure she'll be very very good. . . . She'll be twenty soon, and I was about that age when I started. It's obviously difficult to start with, but you just have to take the plunge.'

Diana agreed, 'I'll just take it as it comes.' And when Grania Forbes commented on her poise and confidence, she said that it was 'marvellous' to have Prince Charles's support. 'It's always nice when there are two of you and there's someone there to help you.'

The one topic she needed no encouragement to talk about, however, was her engagement ring. She was as pleased as punch with it, even though she did try to hide her bitten nails. She had chosen it herself – all £28,500 of it – from Garrard &

Co., the Crown Jewellers in Regent Street. It was a large oval sapphire surrounded by fourteen diamonds set on a platinum shank, a surprisingly traditional design, copies of which went on sale in just about every gift and jewellery shop in the land within days.

After lunch with the Queen and Prince Andrew, Diana changed into a new outfit for a photo-call on the terrace and lawn at the back of Buckingham Palace. It was the first time that she had willingly posed for a photographer since she had stood in her see-through skirt outside the kindergarten five months earlier, yet in those intervening five months she had become the most-photographed person in Britain.

Then there was another interview, the one Diana had been dreading most of all, for television. She couldn't bear the way she looked on television, and whenever she saw herself she used to hide her head in her hands and groan: 'Oh God, I look awful. Why did I say that?'

Despite her foreboding it went well. Once again there were no unexpected questions; Keith Graves of the BBC and Anthony Carthew of ITN repeated much the same questions as Diana and Charles had been asked in the morning.

Diana's reply to the question of what she and Charles had in common, was their sense of humour and every outdoor activity, 'Except I don't ride. Lots of things really.' Charles remarked that he would soon remedy the fact that she didn't ride. When pressed to give his version of what they had in common, Charles said, 'Certainly all sorts of things. . . . Our love of the outdoors. And she's a very energetic character as well – which is very encouraging. Music and interests like that, and skiing. She's a great skier – although I haven't seen her skiing yet.'

To sum up they were asked to find words for the way they felt that day. 'Difficult to find the words, really,' began Charles, then turning to Diana said, 'Isn't it? Just delighted and happy. I'm amazed that she's been brave enough to take me on.'

'And I suppose in love?' ventured the interviewers.

'Of course!' said Diana without a moment's hesitation, while Charles was a little less hasty. 'Whatever "in love"

112

means,' he said, giving just about every women's page writer food for thought.

If Diana had had any nails at the beginning of that day she had none by the end. It was a nerve-wracking ordeal, but exhilarating too: the activity outside Buckingham Palace; the cheering of the crowds; the excitement of everyone inside the Palace; the popping of champagne corks and the look of unadulterated enthusiasm on every face she saw.

She had come through it with flying colours; but she had also embarked on a whole new way of life. Scotland Yard detectives, including Paul Officer and John Maclean, had been assigned to act as her bodyguards from 11 o'clock that morning *ad infinitum*. Wherever she goes in public, whether she walks, drives or skis, whether she is with Prince Charles, a Latin lover or by herself, one of them will be with her.

She moved out of Coleherne Court on the Monday afternoon and apart from going back with her detective to collect a few more personal items two days later, she only ever returned as a visitor.

And as she shut the door on the last kitchen sink and the last ironing board she would ever have to stand over, or the last Hoover that she would plug in for herself, she left a poignant note for her flatmates, giving them her new telephone number: 'For God's sake ring me up – I'm going to need you.'

With that she was swept away to stay with the Queen Mother at Clarence House, leaving observers lamenting about what she had shut the door on. One such lament came 'With love and good wishes from the *Harpers & Queen* piper':

> *Goodbye to hearing the doorbell and going to find out*
> *Goodbye to being able to drink so much you wipe out*
> *Goodbye.*
> *Goodbye to looking as bad as you feel*
> *Goodbye to queueing for a table in Geale's*
> *Goodbye.*
> *Goodbye to not knowing what you'll do today*
> *Goodbye to bargains and what you can afford to pay*
> *Goodbye.*
> *Goodbye to running to jump on the bus*
> *Goodbye to mistreatment and making a fuss*

Goodbye.
Goodbye to cooking and Sqezying the plates
Goodbye to boasting about crushes and hates
Goodbye.
Goodbye to thinking you are liked for yourself
Goodbye to garlic and risking your health
Goodbye.
Goodbye to being able to trust anybody
Goodbye to private ownership of your body
Goodbye.
Goodbye to nineteen years of freedom and beauty
Embrace duty.

It was a lament that was lost on Diana. She was saying goodbye to most of those things with the greatest of pleasure; and those she would miss, things which all the ponderous observers of royal behaviour had predicted that she would have to give up, she had no intention of saying goodbye to at all. Nor did she. From that first day she came under the umbrella of royalty, she made it perfectly plain she was nobody's yes-man.

Diana didn't actually stay at Clarence House for long. She was given a suite of rooms at Buckingham Palace, which the Royal Family felt would be livelier and less old-fashioned for a nineteen-year-old than the Queen Mother's residence, and so the Palace became her base. But, in fact, she led a rather nomadic existence for the next five months up to the wedding. She spent a lot of time at Kensington Palace with her sister Jane, who was someone she knew she could confide in. Since growing up Diana had been closer to Jane than anyone else in her family, and Jane could now provide positive support since, with Robert's role as the Queen's Assistant Private Secretary, she knew all the ropes herself. Another person upon whom she relied heavily in the months ahead – for many of which Charles was away – was her mother. They went together on shopping sprees and to dress fittings, and while she was in London, Diana frequently stayed with her at her flat in Warwick Square.

In some ways life had become easier since the engagement had been announced. In other ways it was more of a strain than ever. The newspapers devoted more column inches to Diana than ever before, and sought out everyone from psychologists and genealogists to friends, cousins and old family retainers to say their pennyworth. Reporters invaded the villages around Althorp, and the schools that Diana had attended, getting in through the back door with the bread delivery man in one case, trying to climb in through a lavatory window in another, and ringing their telephones incessantly, until a great many of these people who had never spoken to a journalist in their lives were afraid to open their own front doors.

About the most scandalous story the press eventually came up with was told by a butler at Althorp, Mr Pendry, who revealed that Diana had been skinny-dipping in the pool one night in the midst of a party. The French magazine, *Paris Match*, managed to procure some rather daring photographs of Diana aged seventeen, standing in the snow wrapped in a towel and flaunting a bra in one hand, taken on a skiing holiday in France.

No one got very far on the theme of ex-lovers. One suggested candidate was James Boughey, a young army officer and old Etonian; others thought Rory Scott, a lieutenant in the Scots Guards, more likely on the grounds that Diana had washed and ironed his shirts for him. What they failed to appreciate was that Diana was a frustrated Chinese laundrymaid in those days, and would gladly have washed anybody's shirts.

Such speculations didn't produce a lover, but they did secure a most extraordinary statement from Diana's uncle, Lord Fermoy, who appeared to have set himself up as an authority on Diana's love life, despite being one of the least close of her relatives. 'Diana, I can assure you,' he said, 'has never had a lover. To my knowledge she has never been involved in that way with anyone.'

Even the Communist-controlled *Morning Star* thought that statement beyond the pale. In an article headlined 'Don't do it, Lady Diana', it pointed out that she was 'to sacrifice her independence to a domineering layabout for the sake of a few lousy foreign holidays'. But it went on to say that 'Any illusions Lady Diana may have about being a person, the owner of her own body and sexuality, should have been sharply shattered by her father and uncle who have publicly guaranteed their valuable commodity will be delivered to the Prince in a state of unsullied innocence.' 'The "suitable bride" treatment she has received at the hands of the press and even her own family degrades not only her,' it concluded, 'but all women.'

Diana was upset that the subject of her virginity was being bandied about, but the *Morning Star*'s blow for feminism was falling on deaf ears. All Diana wanted out of life was a husband and children whom she could love and look after, and who would love and look after her. If she was throwing away independence in exchange for that, then who wanted independence?

She was also, of course, taking on more than 'a few lousy foreign holidays'. There's no doubt that Diana was marrying for love of Charles, but she would have been a very abnormal girl if she wasn't also slightly in love with the Charles who was Prince of Wales, Duke of Cornwall, one of the richest men in Britain, and one of the most famous men in the world. Furthermore, had she not been a little bit in love with the Prince in him the prospect of being a Princess herself, she would have been quite wrong for the job. And the fact of the matter was that she was perfect for the job.

The 'Shy Di' that the newspapers had monotonously called her grew very quickly into a glamorous young woman, and it wasn't just new clothes and the Palace that did it. Being engaged had brought security and confidence. She was transformed in much the same way as during the months she had worked at the kindergarten, where she had found that she was wanted and needed.

Ever since she was a child, Diana has always had strong will, strong character and a toughness that she had inherited from her mother. When she has wanted something in her life she has got it. If she has made up her mind to do something, she has done it. The shy quality, which was much more a lack of confidence than a fear of people, grew directly from her basic sense of insecurity – the insecurity of a child from a broken home. Once she was given security, which she herself said that she had felt for the first time in her life on becoming engaged to

116

Charles, then she began to blossom. And all those around her were suddenly forced to sit up and take notice.

The world did that quite literally on her first official public engagement with Charles after the announcement: a charity gala of verse and music at the Goldsmiths' Hall in the City of London. Diana arrived in a dramatically low-cut, strapless black silk ballgown, which appeared to be held up by the grace of God and nothing else. It was a far far cry from the demure high-necked, ruffled, whiter-than-white styles she had chosen in the past. When she bent down to climb out of the car as it drew up to the Goldsmiths' Hall no one dared breathe for fear the lady would lose her all.

More significant than the evening dress was the fact that the next day Buckingham Palace announced that the couple who had designed it, David and Elizabeth Emanuel, had been chosen to make Diana's wedding dress. It was a bold statement that she was running her own show. Many people had expected her to choose the Queen's dress designer, Norman Hartnell.

Diana had first encountered the Emanuels' work at Lord Snowdon's small studio in Kensington, where she had gone to be photographed for *Vogue*. She took a particular liking to the blouse that she was given to wear, which was her sort of style: pink chiffon with a high frilled neck. It turned out to have been made by the Emanuels. A few days later Diana rang *Vogue* to ask how she could get in touch with the Emanuels, and was given their number. When she announced herself as Diana Spencer, they thought it must be some sort of joke, they couldn't believe it was *the* Diana Spencer. However, she made an appointment with them at their side-alley salon in Brook Street, where people like Bianca Jagger, Lulu, Arianna Stassinopoulos and Susan Hampshire shop, and by February had become quite a regular customer.

Their theme has always been romantic, and when asked why, David Emanuel explained, 'One needs romance in the climate in which we live. To me, if there is the excuse to dress up, you should dress up. It is very sad not to bother. And for anyone who insists on being sloppy, well, then, she can dress down divinely.'

Diana never showed any inclination to be sloppy. Her

117

choice in the clothes that she wore became more and more classy as she found a new way of shopping. Now that she was a well-known figure, Diana found it awkward to hunt for clothes. She couldn't just stride into the shops that she used to go to; places like Laura Ashley, Fiorucci or Benetton, which were always milling with people. Even Harrods and Harvey Nichols were difficult, although she did continue to use them both and still does. She had developed a yen for more distinctive clothes but she found it embarrassing to go into the deathly hush of a designer showroom, particularly if she was 'just looking'.

Vogue magazine had the answer. Diana's sister Jane had worked there as an editorial assistant before she was married, and as a result she still had friends working on the magazine whom she could trust to be discreet. As a top fashion magazine they knew all the designers, and what was available in the shops; and regularly each month dozens of outfits and accessories came into the fashion department at their offices in Hanover Square, for possible use in the magazine. Diana was able to go along, and in total privacy view and try on all the most exclusive, most fashionable clothes. She could then be sure when she contacted a designer that she was going to want to buy what he had to offer.

She also had the benefit of expert fashion advice from some top people in the business: Beatrix Miller, Editor-in-Chief of the magazine; Grace Coddington, the Fashion Editor, once a well-known model; and Anna Harvey, the Deputy Fashion Editor. They were able to help Diana decide what suited her, what would be suitable for which occasion, and what accessories to match up with. To begin with Diana was going into *Vogue* two or three times a week. Not only did she need outfits for her engagements up to the wedding, she also had to choose clothes for her trousseau, and for the weeks that would be spent in Scotland after the honeymoon.

With her experience as a model, Grace Coddington was able to offer a few professional tips on walking in front of crowds of people and cameras, and on general deportment. Like a lot of tall girls, Diana had a habit of walking and standing as though she were trying to make herself look a couple of inches shorter, and having a fiancé who was almost exactly the same height in bare feet – 5 ft 10 ins – didn't help.

The Beauty Editor, Felicity Clark, gave Diana professional advice on her make-up. Diana had never worn much at all, but now she was going to be in the public eye more than ever, and had become a tireless subject for criticism and appraisal from not only British, but foreign newspapers and magazines as well, she needed some help.

If Diana needed some expert advice with her appearance, she needed none whatsoever in dealing with people. She proved to be more of a 'natural' on walkabouts than any other member of the Royal Family with the exception of the Queen Mother, who had, of course, come from a similar kind of background. She talked to people with such friendliness and charm that everyone she met felt at ease. And the effect was tumultuous.

One of the first times that she was put to the test was at Cheltenham, where she and Prince Charles were visiting the headquarters of the Gloucestershire Police, into whose patch Highgrove falls. They had arrived by helicopter – with Charles at the controls – and as usual the whole area was crowded with cheering people. Amongst them was a bold sixth-form schoolboy, who held out an offering of a single daffodil. As Diana took the daffodil, he looked her straight in the eye and said: 'May I kiss the hand of my future Queen?' 'Of course you may,' said Diana, and added, blushing as crimson as her future subject, 'You'll never live this down!'

Charles spent that afternoon with his present Queen, at a meeting of the Privy Council in the White Drawing Room at Buckingham Palace, for the solemn business of obtaining her formal consent to his marriage.

Solemnity duly over, the Queen posed for the first photographs that had ever been taken of her with her son and future daughter-in-law. She wasn't playing Monarch now, she was playing proud mother, and showing the world that she had no doubts whatsoever that Charles had picked a perfect bride.

The British public were in no doubt that he had too, and watching Diana say goodbye to Charles on the tarmac at Heathrow Airport two days later brought a lump to even the most sceptical throat, as he left for a five-week tour on the other side of the world. She was brave as he grasped her arm and kissed her, but as she stood in the wind and the rain, watching his plane taxi away, she broke down and cried and her public loved her all the more.

He may have taken off for the other side of the world – first stop New Zealand, and from there to Australia, Venezuela and America, but Charles telephoned Diana every single day. This made it all the more credible when news broke in Australia that his conversations with the Queen and with Diana had been tapped and taped, and worse still, that they had been sold to the German magazine *Die Aktuelle*, who were determined to publish them.

Fortunately Charles was back by the time the story hit Britain. He immediately took legal action to prevent the transcripts being published in Britain, and was granted an interim injunction in the High Court. As it turned out, the tapes were phoney anyway, but the injunction saved a lot of unnecessary embarrassment.

Soon after Charles had left on this five-week tour – where he was haunted by Lady Diana look-alikes everywhere he turned – Buckingham Palace announced the first details of the wedding plans, and the souvenir merchants were in business.

Despite a three-page ruling from the Lord Chamberlain that the souvenirs were to be in good taste, which meant no royal arms or royal photographs to appear on T-shirts, the industry went wild. In no time at all almost every shop window in every town and village in the country was displaying Charles and Diana tea-towels, T-shirts, tea-caddies, trays, jigsaw puzzles, playing cards, mugs, glasses, decanters, plates, lighters, ashtrays, place-mats and teaspoons. The list was endless, and no one grew more tired of seeing her face plastered over everything than Diana herself.

One weekend while she was down at Althorp staying with her father, Diana offered to drive Betty Andrew, the housekeeper and ladies' maid, home to her cottage in Great Brington. She should, of course, have taken her detective too; but Diana managed to give him the slip and sped away to the village which was not much more than a mile away from the house. Betty's front door was one along from the village post office and shop which, like every other shop for miles around, was full of wedding souvenirs. Before going in to greet Betty's husband Ted, Diana popped into the shop to try to buy herself an ice-lolly.

'It's *not*,' said the owner, aghast at seeing Diana standing in his shop and dressed in jeans and a Guernsey sweater just like any other customer. He could hardly believe his eyes.

'It *is*', assured Betty, his next-door neighbour.

'Oh, my wife will be furious that she wasn't here to see you,' he said at last. Diana asked where his wife was.

'She's out buying more mugs with pictures of you on them to put in the shop!' he said, at which Diana giggled and said, 'Oh, God, I'm sorry.'

That same weekend she treated all the staff in the kitchen at Althorp to a private view of the jewellery that she had worn at Ascot. They had already ogled her engagement ring. While Charles was abroad she had driven down one weekend to Althorp in his Aston Martin. She had been like a little kid showing off a new toy; she even took the ring off and let all the women try it on their own fingers. Betty very nearly couldn't get it off again, and lived through the longest thirty seconds that she's ever been through, with the future Queen of England's £28,500 engagement ring stuck on her finger.

Ascot had been a great excuse for dressing up, but she had never really enjoyed any sort of horsey event, and racing least of all. At weekend house parties that she had been to in the past, point-to-points were frequently on the agenda for Saturday afternoons, and Diana had always been too polite to say anything, but she had gone to them under sufferance.

Moreover, she hasn't been endeared to racing by her association with Prince Charles, but rather confirmed in her belief, since her own fall from a pony at Park House in her youth when she broke her arm, that horses pose a threat to life and limb. After the tragedy of Allibar's heart attack, Charles took a couple of hefty falls in the space of five days: the first steeple-chasing at Sandown, where he fell off his new horse, Good Prospect, at the eighteenth fence; the second at Cheltenham in the Kim Muir Memorial Challenge Cup, where it was the tenth fence that got him.

The next sporting event in the calendar was much more up

Diana's street: Wimbledon. She had been a faithful fan for years, never missing the first Saturday, to which her mother always used to take her from school. Unless she was lucky enough to get a ticket for any other day she spent the rest of the fortnight glued to the television. But in 1981 she had the best view ever – from the royal box – for the three most exciting days in the whole tournament, the Thursday, Friday and Saturday of the last week: the semi-finals and finals of all the competitions.

But along with the perks came a few gentle reminders of what the job she was about to sign up for, for the rest of her life, was all about. She planted her first tree at Broadlands, Lord Romsey's home in Hampshire, where she and Charles were to spend the first night of their honeymoon. She lunched at Windsor along with the Queen, the Duke of Edinburgh and Charles, with the President of Ghana, and went to a dedication service in the parish church at Tetbury. There were banquets too, like one given by the Queen at Buckingham Palace for King Khaled of Saudi Arabia, and his return offering at Claridges.

She had to duck out of a few engagements too, for time was pressing. There were wedding dress fittings, and she hadn't helped matters by losing nearly a stone in weight between February, when she was first measured for the dress, and July. There were the bridesmaids' dresses to choose and organize, lists to make, invitations to write, and forty-seven thousand letters to answer, not to mention the ten thousand presents that needed thank-yous.

To ensure that they weren't given ten thousand toast racks, and to help people stuck for ideas, Diana made up a wedding list at the General Trading Company off Sloane Square, and Thomas Goode, the Mayfair china experts. Between them the two London shops provided everything from the purely practical to the frankly fanciful, with prices to match. But the lists were only shown to people who were invited to the wedding, and the vast majority of presents that Diana and Charles received came from the general public.

The result was that a large portion of Diana's day was spent sitting at a small table in a small room shared with Oliver

'I cannot believe Lady Di does not like riding!'

Everett, a diplomat who had been recalled from Madrid to work as Diana's personal private secretary. Six Wrens, brought in specially to help with the letters and presents that flooded into Buckingham Palace, were closeted away in another room upstairs.

Letters or presents from people that Diana knew personally, she answered herself, by hand. They were not just brief notes, but thoughtful newsy letters, saying what she would do with the present, how excited she was, how busy, and how she was looking forward to setting up home at Highgrove. Diana was obviously well aware that these were letters that people were going to keep, treasure and produce for their children and their children's children.

She gave one of her engagement presents to Betty Andrew at Althorp. It wasn't planned: she opened it up and on the spur of the moment said, 'Here, Betty, you have it, and keep it for ever,' knowing that it would sit, as it does, in pride of place inside a glass cabinet in the Andrews' living room, to be brought out and shown to every visitor.

In between answering letters, dress fittings, shoe fittings, shopping and official engagements, dinners, garden parties and gala premieres, Diana also found time to go back to the kindergarten to see her friends and the children there. If she had ever been suffering from any delusions of grandeur, the children brought her straight back to earth. They were thrilled to see her, but treated her in exactly the same way as they had before. Most of them still called her Miss Diana, although a few had picked up the Lady Diana tag, after hearing it so much on television. One child had heard so much about the wedding that he was convinced that anyone with the name Charles had the prefix Prince, and is probably still to this day referring to a rather surprised little mite in the school as Prince Charles.

She also took up dancing again. It was obviously difficult for her to join a class at the Dance Centre any more, and so she approached Wendy Vickers, who had taught her to dance at West Heath, and asked her to give her private lessons at Buckingham Palace. So, two mornings a week, Wendy would arrive at the Palace with her pianist, Alice Elliott. Diana brushed up her ballet, ending up each session with tap, and dancing to songs like 'Hello Dolly', and the Fred Astaire classics, 'Teach the World to Sing', and 'Top Hat, White Tie and Tails'. After the strain of the publicity, the tedium of letter writing and the pressures of the wedding preparations, it was an escape. She could put everything out of her mind for a couple of hours and lose herself in a world of her own: something she had been able to do by dancing ever since she was a child.

As 29 July drew nearer, the strain of it all finally began to show. When crowds surrounded her at a polo match one afternoon at Tidworth, where she had gone to watch Charles play, she broke down and ran off in tears. The next morning newspaper stories abounded about how Diana hated polo and everything to do with horses, how she was ill, how she was cracking up under the strain of it all.

Her likes or dislikes of the game had very little to do with it, nor was she cracking up. Diana was quite simply exhausted and, like most brides five days before their wedding, was growing increasingly nervous of the day ahead. She had had to prepare for the ceremony under the constant gaze of the world's press. Every day there were newspaper articles about her, interviews with her friends, her teachers, some true, some not, and a lot of what she read upset her. The strain of ten months in the limelight, in a way no one has ever been in the limelight before, was beginning to take its toll.

But Diana was not, as her teachers at Riddlesworth Hall had observed, 'ever a one to have boo-hooed'. She recovered herself quickly and the next day she was back watching Charles play polo again, getting straight back into the saddle again, so to speak.

By Monday she was into the final furlong. The Queen gave a dinner party at Buckingham Palace that night for relatives and close friends, at which Diana's mother and father were together with their respective spouses. After dinner guests moved on to a vast reception and dance, and were sent away in the wee small hours of the morning each clutching a giant balloon bearing the Prince of Wales feathers.

The next night the nation joined in the fun, with a giant firework display in Hyde Park and beacons lit throughout the land. But the one person not out on the streets on that exciting night was Diana. she was staying with the Queen Mother at Clarence House, for her last hours as Lady Diana Spencer. Even if she didn't sleep, she went to bed for an early night while the beacons burned, and the capital rejoiced and prepared for royal wedding day.

THE WEDDING

ON 26 JULY 1981, a Sunday, the very day that Diana Spencer was showing a brave face on the polo field at Windsor, stifling her nerves about the ordeal of the forthcoming Wednesday, the first sightseers were arriving in London and setting up camp to be sure of a good view of the wedding procession as it passed on its way to St Paul's Cathedral. They were a teacher and her daughter from Somerset, and a salesman from Cannock in Staffordshire, who sat themselves down in the Mall on deckchairs borrowed from St James's Park, and listened patiently as every passer-by stopped to tell them kindly that the wedding wasn't until Wednesday. 'If you're going to be a fanatic, you might as well do a good job of it', one of them stoutly maintained.

Two more fanatics had pitched camp further along the route, in Fleet Street, one of the busiest thoroughfares in London. They were two housewives from Thirsk in Yorkshire, and for two days and three nights they sat on the edge of the pavement with sleeping bags and two carriers full of food, laughing cheerfully while heavy lorries, buses and weekday traffic thundered past, belching fumes at them.

Thousands of people had swarmed into London that Sunday to watch the Horse Guards and the carriages rehearse the route that they would take to the Cathedral. The traffic, normally very quiet on a Sunday, was far busier than a normal rush hour, and not helped by people stopping their cars and climbing out to take historic photographs. Fifteen thousand people are thought to have visited St Paul's that day, just to see for themselves the place where Charles and Diana were to be married. The streets around the Cathedral were jammed until late into the night. Wedding fever had begun.

On that same afternoon London's Oxford Street hosted the biggest tea party in the world. Thousands of children, mostly disabled or from broken homes, sat down at eight hundred and sixty-one tables which stretched for one and a quarter miles, ate five thousand hamburgers and toasted Prince Charles and Lady Diana with eight hundred gallons of soft drinks.

On Tuesday, while the wedding cake was delivered to Buckingham Palace, and the dress to Clarence House, half a million people converged on Hyde Park for the fireworks, and thousands more crowded around the hundreds of beacons on high ground all over England, Scotland and Wales. At 10.08 p.m. precisely Prince Charles set a torch to the first beacon and the celebrations began. The firework display was based on similar celebrations held two hundred years earlier for the Peace of Aix-la-Chapelle, and was stunning in its effect. As rockets whizzed and banged and multi-coloured stars filled the sky, the massed bands of the Household musicians struck up, and the Morrison Orpheus Choir and the Choir of the Welsh Guards burst into song while above all the Royal Horse Artillery fired salvoes from the guns of the King's Troop.

The streets of London were alive throughout the hot July night. Thousands of people set off on the long walk back to their cars or to their homes, while thousands more with sleeping bags flocked towards the Mall, Trafalgar Square, the Strand, Fleet Street, and up Ludgate Hill to the Cathedral, to lay claim to a viewpoint. Students from Trinity College, Cambridge, where Prince Charles had been a student, wore evening dress and sat down to a candle-lit dinner as they waited on the pavement in the Mall.

At 4 a.m. the route was closed to traffic, by dawn there was no standing room to be had within a hundred yards of St Paul's, and by 9 o'clock, when the first guests started to climb the red-carpeted steps to the great west doors, more than a million people were spread out along the wedding route. Most of them would get the barest glimpse for their pains, but that didn't seem to bother any one of them. They had come with camping stoves and thermos flasks, sandwiches and beer and champagne. They had come to have a party, to see a fairy-tale come true, and they chattered to everyone around them, to friends and strangers alike, and cheered and waved and wept and sang.

Four thousand police lined the route too, the same men and women who just a few weeks before had stood bloodied and battered behind riot shields in Liverpool, London and Manchester. But today, those same members of the public who had been bombarding them with broken bottles and bricks were showering them with gifts of crisps, sweets and hot drinks.

There were closed-circuit television cameras to monitor every inch of the procession route, there were special constables, uniformed and plain-clothed men, cadets, mounted police and the St John Ambulance Brigade on hand. A Metropolitan Police helicopter kept a watch from the air, and marksmen were stationed on the roof tops, providing round-the-clock protection to nearly two hundred VIP guests: and a Special Branch man disguised in royal livery and armed with a ·36 Smith and Wesson hand gun rode 'shotgun' on the back of Prince Charles's open carriage.

But nothing marred the day. Two telephone calls warning that fire bombs had been planted in St Paul's were quickly discounted as hoaxes, and police made no more than ten arrests, most of those for pickpocketing. At the end of it all, the police chiefs from both the City of London and the Metropolitan forces thanked the crowds for 'making the only memory which will stay with us one of joy'.

It was a day of joy for everyone, from the bride to the millions of people watching her on television all over the world; and it was a very determined person who failed to be moved by the roar of the crowds, the colour, the music, the laughter and the excitement of everyone who was there with her.

Diana's day began soon after 6 o'clock in her suite at Clarence House with a normal breakfast of coffee. The usual quiet of the Queen Mother's residence was shattered that morning. The bridesmaids all had to be dressed and prepared, Diana had to have her hair done, her face made up and get into her own dress all before she and her father were due to leave for the Cathedral, just after 10.30 a.m.

Diana was excited and nervous by turns, but no more so than her helpers. Her hairdresser, Kevin Shanley, had come armed with no fewer than ten hairbrushes, ten combs and three hairdryers – just in case one of them blew up. The Emanuels had two replicas of the wedding dress, lest there was a disaster of some sort with the original.

Kevin was the first person to arrive at Clarence House, accompanied by his wife Claire, also a hairdresser, who was to help with the bridesmaids' hair. He styled Diana's hair just as she always wore it, with the fringe falling softly to one side, so that she should feel as comfortable and natural as possible.

Her make-up, put on by Barbara Daly, was also as natural as she normally wore it. Barbara Daly, who had been recommended by the Beauty Editor at *Vogue* and is recognized as one of the top make-up artists in the country, had already had a few dummy runs with Diana's face for some of her previous public engagements, so she was confident of the colours that suited her best. Barbara normally takes two hours to put on full-face make-up, but it took her no more than forty-five minutes to apply the amount that Diana wanted. Diana's complexion is almost flawless, with its 'peaches and cream' colouring and, as everyone had noted long ago, she has no need for any kind of artificial blusher.

Barbara also manicured Diana's nails that morning and painted them with a clear gloss. Once they were well and truly dry, it was the Emanuels' turn to sew the final stitches on their creation in the superstitious belief that it's lucky to sew the last stitch when the bride is wearing her gown.

Their dress was a sensation: an elaborate, billowing ocean of ivory silk paper taffeta, hand embroidered in tiny mother-of-pearl sequins and pearls, with ornate panels back and front, and with lace-flounced sleeves and a neckline decorated with taffeta bows. Behind flowed a twenty-five-foot train of the same silk taffeta, trimmed and edged with sparkling old lace. The silk had come from Britain's last remaining silk farm, Lullingstone in Dorset, where locals had been scouring the countryside week after week for the mulberry leaves to feed the tens of thousands of silkworms that were spinning away for Queen and Country.

Despite the secrecy and the desperate lengths of espionage,

even bribery, that some fashion magazines had gone to to try and get a preview of the dress, the Emanuels revealed once it was all over that Diana had chosen a design which they had created for a fashion show in London some time before, which most fashion writers had already seen, and which had been shown to Diana on a video recording. The design had even been featured in *Vogue*, although the colour was different and the train and various other details had been added specifically for Diana.

But the dress nevertheless remained the best kept secret of the wedding. Details had been strictly embargoed until 10.35 on the morning of the wedding, the precise moment when Diana's Glass Coach left Clarence House. No one had a proper view of the dress in all its glory until she stepped out on to the steps of St Paul's just before 11 o'clock. Yet four hours later, after they had first seen the dress on their televisions, a London bridal-fashion firm in the East End had finished a simplified version, and within five hours copies of the dress were on sale in the shops.

The copies sold at a fraction of the price of the original. Diana's dress, complete with the train and veil, cost over £2,000, although she was never actually charged for it. The publicity that the Emanuels received as a result of making the dress was worth infinitely more, and they were only too glad to give it to her.

It was an outfit for a princess, completed by the Spencer family diamond tiara which held Diana's veil in place and gleamed and sparkled in the brilliant lights of the Cathedral, and diamond earrings borrowed from her mother. She completed the superstitious rhyme, 'Something old, something new, something borrowed, something blue' with her own sapphire and diamond engagement ring, which she wore on the third finger of her right hand before she was married, and quickly moved to the third finger of her left hand to sit beside her shining new wedding ring after the vows.

The wedding ring had been delivered to Charles at Buckingham Palace in a little grey suede bag with a drawstring top during the previous week. It was made out of the same piece of gold that had provided the wedding rings of the Queen Mother, the Queen, Princess Margaret and Princess Anne: a

Diana enjoyed the excuse to dress up for Ascot, but horse-racing had never held much interest

Left: The Queen posing with Charles and Diana after giving formal consent to the marriage. Left, below: Charles and Diana emerging from St Paul's Cathedral after their wedding. Right: The Prince and Princess, happy and relaxed, on their honeymoon at Balmoral. Below: Gibraltarians cheering the royal honeymooners

Above: The royal tour of Wales.
Despite the pouring rain,
crowds waited for hours to see
and even touch the Princess.
Right: The Princess, dressed in
the red, white and green of
Wales, giving her husband a
sparkling sidelong glance

Left: Diana arriving at
the opening of the London
Film Festival on 4 November
1981, two days before she told
the world that she was
pregnant. Right: Pressmen
hounded Diana even in the
streets of Tetbury, near her
home at Highgrove

Above: The first public appearance of Prince William, as the Princess leaves the Lindo Wing of St Mary's Paddington less than twenty-four hours after the birth of her son. Left: The christening took place at Buckingham Palace on 4 August 1982. Prince William is held by his proud great-grandmother, flanked by the Prince of Wales and the Queen. Right: The Princess of Wales leaving St Paul's Cathedral after the Falkland Islands Service, 26 July 1982

Prince William, aged seventeen months,
on his first royal walkabout in the
grounds of Kensington Palace. His
proud parents look on

nugget of twenty-two carat gold found at Clogau St David's mine in North Wales more than fifty years before. Collingwood's, the Conduit Street jewellers, had used the last of it on Diana's ring.

Prince Charles looked magnificent too. He has always looked best in uniform, and he was married in the full dress uniform of a Royal Navy commander, with a splendid blue Garter sash. He travelled to St Paul's in the same 1902 State postillion landau that was to carry him home with his bride; but for the outward journey his companion was his brother Andrew, also dressed in naval uniform, but that of his own rank, a midshipman.

Charles had no best man, but two 'supporters' instead, his two brothers, Andrew and Edward. It was Andrew as the principal supporter who performed the tasks usually assigned to the best man: producing the ring in church and proposing the toast at the reception afterwards.

Diana had seven attendants – five bridesmaids and two page boys. They were all known to her, but were either Charles's relations or the children of his friends. All the bridesmaids wore dresses designed by the Emanuels, and the younger ones wore garlands of flowers in their hair.

Chief bridesmaid, who kept all the others and Diana's twenty-five foot train in order, was Princess Margaret's seventeen-year-old daughter, Lady Sarah Armstrong-Jones, also Charles's first cousin. She was by no means unknown to Diana. When the Spencers were living at Park House Lady Sarah would occasionally come over with her cousins to play; she was also bridesmaid to Diana's sister, Sarah and, in recent months, Diana and Lady Sarah had become close friends.

Two of the bridesmaids were Charles's goddaughters: India Hicks, aged thirteen, granddaughter of Lord Mountbatten, and daughter of David Hicks, the interior designer; and six-year-old Catherine Cameron, the eldest daughter of Donald Cameron of Lochiel and Lady Cecil Kerr.

Sarah-Jane Gaselee, eleven, was Charles's trainer's daughter, whom Diana had met several times when she had been breakfasting at Lambourne after Charles's early morning gallops.

The youngest bridesmaid, and the one with whom millions

of people fell in love on the day of the wedding, was five-year-old Clementine Hambro, great-granddaughter of Sir Winston Churchill. She was also the one that Diana knew best, for she had taught her at the Young England Kindergarten.

The two page boys, dressed in 1863 naval uniform, were Edward van Cutsem, the eight-year-old son of Charles's millionaire racehorse training friends, Hugh and Emilie van Cutsem; and his godson, Lord Nicholas Windsor, the Duke and Duchess of Kent's younger son, aged eleven.

St Paul's was packed. Guests had been entering since the west doors opened at 9 o'clock, and each arrival had been greeted with a rousing cheer from the crowds.

In all, 2,650 invitations had been sent out by the Lord Chamberlain, who, as head of the Royal Household, is responsible for the organization of state visits, and of Court Ceremonies, such as royal weddings and funerals.

The majority of the invitations had gone to servants of the Crown and State: senior members of the services, diplomats, and politicians – Mrs Thatcher with her husband, Edward Heath and Harold Macmillan – civil servants, heads of industry, local government officials and over two hundred members of the Queen's staff from Sandringham, Balmoral and Windsor.

Most of the crowned heads of Europe were present, with the notable exception of Charles's friend, Juan Carlos of Spain, who with his Queen had boycotted the wedding for political reasons, because Charles and Diana were not prepared to change their plans about joining the royal yacht at Gibraltar.

But the wedding was attended by the King and Queen of the Belgians, the King and Queen of Sweden, the King of Norway, the Queen of The Netherlands, the Grand Duke and Duchess of Luxembourg and Princess Grace of Monaco with her son, Crown Prince Albert. There were innumerable monarchs from Africa, the Middle East and Asia, and the twenty-five-stone King of Tonga, for whom an extra-large chair had been made.

There were over 160 foreign presidents, prime ministers and their wives packed into the pews, including Mrs Nancy

Reagan, the wife of the President of the United States, who had arrived in London with twelve security men and five hat boxes, and had declared that the week she was going to spend in Britain was the longest period she had been away from her husband in twenty-nine years of marriage.

There were also people from the media in St Paul's, not only from all over Britain but from all over the world. Television crews were perched on scaffolding in the roof, photographers were squatting in the Whispering Gallery, roasting in the heat of the arc lamps, and pen-pushing reporters were packed like sardines in the body of the cathedral below.

The royal wedding was the biggest and most expensive live Outside Broadcast ever made, said to have cost Britain's own television companies half a million pounds each. Independent television coverage began at 7.30 in the morning, with forty cameras stationed along the route, nine of them inside St Paul's. The BBC began fifteen minutes later, and their programme involved sixty cameras and three hundred and fifty men, and continued for seven hours. By 10 o'clock, five minutes before the first members of the Royal Family set out on their journey to St Paul's, more than 250 million people were said to have been listening to the preparations for the wedding on radio, and well over 700 million people were watching it on television, received by satellite in seventy nations.

But for all the spectators, there were plenty of personal friends amongst the guests too. Diana had been given five hundred invitations for her own friends and relations, and her parents had been given fifty each to distribute. The prominence of Diana's three flatmates, side by side in a row at the front, closer than Nancy Reagan and many other dignitaries, was an indication of just whose wedding this was. It may have been organized by the Lord Chamberlain and paid for by the Queen and the taxpayer, but this was the day for which Diana had lived twenty years, and she wasn't going to let her best friends sit at the back for any First Lady.

She invited most of her old school friends from both Riddlesworth and West Heath, as well as Riddy, Ruth Rudge and Miss Allen, the matron from West Heath. She also made certain an invitation went off to old Ally, her governess from Park House, whom she hadn't seen since she was six years old. The old lady was greatly touched, and it is said that when she died just a few weeks before the wedding day, she had the gilt-edged invitation in her hand.

Diana also used her allocation of invitations for the staff at Althorp, which came as a great surprise to them. Earl Spencer had already explained that with so few invitations to hand out himself, he was sadly going to be unable to ask them. But Diana used her own, and Mr and Mrs Andrew, the housekeeper and her husband, Mr and Mrs Smith, the gamekeeper and his wife, Mr and Mrs Pendry, the ex-butler and his wife, and Mr Watters, the Clerk of Works, all travelled down to London by coach for the greatest day of their lives.

Diana had said that 'inviting one's friends and all the people who've helped us' was a way of personalizing what was in many respects a state occasion. She invited all her current set of friends in London, all ten of the people she had worked with at the kindergarten, Patrick Robinson, the little two-year-old she had looked after in Eaton Square, and his parents, who came all the way from America to be there. She also invited Beatrix Miller, Editor-in-Chief of *Vogue*, and the others from the magazine who had been so helpful and discreet – Grace Coddington, Anna Harvey and Felicity Clark – had all been asked to the ball at Buckingham Palace on the Monday night by way of thanks.

One person sadly omitted from everybody's list, no doubt by mistake, was Betty Vacani, in whose dancing studio Diana had passed a short and inglorious term as a student teacher. This omission was all the more puzzling since, as a teacher of royal children, Prince Charles included, she had been invited to every royal wedding and celebration for the last fifty years or more. But Charles had said in an interview that they both gave to television on the eve of the wedding. 'To try to remember everybody has been an absolute nightmare. Even now I suddenly remember somebody that I'd tried hard to remember but didn't. I hope we've got most people.'

There had been great speculation in the gossip columns about where Raine, Diana's step-mother, would be seated and whether Barbara Cartland, her step-grandmother, would be invited at all.

The satirical magazine *Private Eye* had been running a regular fictitious account of the romance between Charles and Diana called *Born to be Queen* by 'Sylvie Krin', which Diana used to read and laugh out loud over, and Barbara Cartland's invitation, according to them, read:

Her Majesty the Queen
and HRH the Duke of Edinburgh
request the pleasure of the company
of Dame Barbara Cartland
at the wedding of
their son Charles
in Westminster Abbey

Your seat is
Row Z No 47
(NB: RESTRICTED VIEW)
Please bring this card with you

In the end Barbara Cartland wasn't invited, despite stories that she had given her invitation to her son, insisting that weddings were for younger people. She watched it all on television at her home in Hertfordshire, and entertained one hundred members of the local St John Ambulance Brigade, of which she is Deputy President, to tea and champagne.

Raine did take a back seat, and Earl Spencer sat beside Mrs Shand Kydd and their children in Diana's family group in the chancel, opposite the Royal Family group of the Queen, Prince Philip, the Queen Mother, Princess Anne, Captain Mark Phillips, Princess Margaret and her son, Viscount Linley.

It was a scene which ten years ago would have been unthinkable for the Queen in her role as Head of the Church of England: a divorced man and his ex-wife sitting side by side, then walking arm in arm after the Archbishop of Canterbury to sign the register. Moreover Princess Margaret's divorced husband, Lord Snowdon, was sitting in Row A with his second wife beside him. But when the statistics indicate that one in three marriages ends in divorce, even the Royal Family has had to change its attitude, although divorce for either the Queen or Prince Charles would still be unthinkable.

The wedding was held in St Paul's because that was where Charles and Diana both wanted to be married, despite opposition from the Establishment. Westminster Abbey has traditionally been the place for royal weddings. The Queen was married there, as was her mother before her, and it was also the scene of the weddings of Princess Alexandra, Princess Margaret and Princess Anne. All the major weddings of this century have been held there, including that of Johnnie and Frances Althorp, Diana's parents, in 1954.

This was one of the very reasons why Diana was against the Abbey. Her own parents' marriage had been a disaster, and she was superstitious enough to want to start her own marriage under a different roof. Charles wasn't sold on Westminster Abbey either. One of his most recent visits had been for Lord Mountbatten's funeral after he was blown up by an IRA bomb in August 1979, and the Abbey inevitably still brought back memories.

Charles therefore suggested St Paul's as an alternative. He liked the building, he had been to it several times in the past and had even preached in it, and he knew the acoustics were excellent. It was also bigger than the Abbey – 'big enough to take one orchestra if not two,' as Charles explained – and also more guests.

There had been one precedent of a royal wedding for the Lord Chamberlain to consider, Arthur, Prince of Wales, the elder son of Henry VII and Elizabeth of York, had married the young Spanish Princess, Catherine of Aragon, in Old St Paul's in 1501. The bride had progressed along the aisle covered with a red cloth, to join the Prince on the dais, wearing 'upon her head a coif of white silk, with a scarf bordered with gold and pearl and precious stones, five inches and a half broad, which veiled a great part of her visage and person. Her gown was very large, both the sleeves and also the body, with many plaits; and beneath the waist, certain round hoops, bearing out the gown from her body after the manner of her country.'

After the ceremony bells rang out in the City of London and the crowds cheered as they rode to the Bishop of Bath's palace for 'a sumptuous feast and plentiful dancings and disguisings' which lasted all day. That night the newly-weds were ceremoniously led to and ensconced in the marriage bed, and the next morning, it is said, the Prince called for a drink 'which heretofore times he was not accustomed to. One of his chamberlains, marvelling, asked him the cause of his drought, at which the prince answered merrily: "I have this night been in the midst of Spain, which is a hot region . . . ".' It is highly improbable that he had been anywhere of the sort: he was fifteen, Catherine was sixteen, and it is widely accepted that when he died less than five months later the marriage had still not been consummated.

But four hundred and eight years on the problems concerning the Lord Chamberlain were to do with costs. The fact that St Paul's was nearly three times further from Buckingham Palace than the Abbey would involve extra security arrangements and transport which would more than double the cost. At a time when nearly three million people were unemployed and the British economy was at an all-time low, the Queen and her councillors were understandably nervous.

Prince Charles was apparently urged 'to think again, if for no other reason than that we are worried that we will not have enough soldiers to line the route properly', to which Charles replied caustically 'well, stand them further apart'.

Stand them further apart is precisely what was done, and apart from predictable criticism from some extreme left-wingers and from the anti-monarchy MP, Willie Hamilton, the nation bore its share of the cost gladly. Some costs were cut. A lot of decorations used for the Queen's Jubilee in 1977 were revamped and used again. But even so, it was the most expensive wedding recorded in British history. The final estimate was £150,000, of which the Queen would have personally paid £30,000. But a lot of the money included in that estimate was spent on the 2,228 soldiers and 4,000 policemen that lined the route, who would have been paid the same amount in the course of a normal working day. On the other hand, by declaring the wedding day a public holiday the amount of money lost to industry must have been enormous.

But an extravaganza was just the tonic Britain needed. It didn't change anything; three million people were still unemployed on 30 July, but it did restore people's faith in the basic niceness of their fellow human beings after the violence and the horror of the previous few months.

Music was a very important part of the day. In the television interview that Charles and Diana had given the day before, the Prince had said that he had always longed for a musical wedding:

I very much wanted to take a hand in the organization from the beginning and I've had great fun organizing the music with a great deal of help from the Director of the Royal College of Music, Sir David Willcocks, whom I've known for some years through the Bach Choir.

We've had a marvellous time getting together three orchestras that I'm patron of and the Bach Choir that I'm President of, and also, very exciting, Kiri te Kanawa, the Maori opera singer, is prepared to sing in the Cathedral.

So I can't wait for the whole thing. I want everybody to come out, you know, having had a marvellous musical and emotional experience.

Charles walked up the nave of the Cathedral to Henry Purcell's *Trumpet Tune*. As he turned into Dean's Aisle at the top there was a roar from the crowds outside marking the arrival of Diana's Glass Coach. The musical and emotional experience was all set to begin.

The State Trumpeters of the Household Cavalry, standing in the porticoes by the west doors, sounded a fanfare to wake the marble dead and, as the Cathedral clock struck eleven, the dramatic opening bars of Jeremiah Clark's *Trumpet Voluntary* sent tingles shooting up and down a multitude of spines. Diana then began her three-and-a-half-minute walk, followed by her bridesmaids and pages.

138

'I told her it's at St Paul's but she says they always have 'em here.'

On one arm she carried her bouquet, made that morning with a cascade of orchids, stephanotis, gardenias, lilies of the valley, freesias, myrtle, veronica and golden Mountbatten roses. On the other arm she all but carried her father, Earl Spencer, who confided afterwards that he had felt very strange and hot as they walked up the long red carpet, and had leant very heavily on Diana for support.

If anyone had any real fears about the wedding, they were for Earl Spencer, who had never been strong since his illness. But he knew how important it was to Diana that he should be the one to give her away, and struggled courageously to do so. He was guided, steadied and helped and although after the service he had to walk out of the Cathedral entirely on his own beside the Queen, she did relax the protocol and allow him to climb into their waiting landau before her.

Having her father to joke with her and to whisper to as she walked up the aisle was a great boost to Diana. Underneath all the diamonds, the thousands of pounds' worth of silk and pearls and lace, she felt like any other bride; a mixture of nerves and excitement. When she finally reached the end of her walk and stepped up on to the dais beside the Prince, and they looked at one another, this vast state ceremony which had taken so many months of planning, and was being watched by 700 million people, suddenly became as intimate as the smallest church wedding.

The service began with the hymn 'Christ is Made the Sure Foundation', which Charles had chosen because he said it had 'the most marvellous harmony,' adding, 'I find it very moving. I shall, I think spend half the time in tears'. He didn't, although there was a hint of a tear glistening on his cheek as the organ crashed out the last notes of the hymn, and he clearly found the whole service very moving.

Diana's choice of hymn was very appropriate, 'I Vow to Thee My Country'. But it wasn't a political choice; this was actually her favourite hymn, and the one that she had chosen as her leaving hymn in her last term at West Heath.

The Dean of St Paul's introduced the service, but it was the Archbishop of Canterbury, Robert Runcie, resplendent in a brand new silk cope, who took them through the marriage vows. 'I don't get much opportunity for weddings,' he had said when he had told the General Synod that he would be officiating at the royal wedding, 'It'll be nice to keep my hand in.' He was the ideal man for the job, sincere without being pompous, and with a sense of humour which appealed to both Charles and Diana.

Unlike past royal brides Diana had decided to leave out the promise to 'obey' her husband in the marriage service. It is left out in most modern ceremonies nowadays but, as Robert Runcie had pointed out to her, 'obey' was a lot better than the promise extracted from brides in the Middle Ages to be 'bonny and buxom, at bed and board'.

Diana promised neither. She made the simply vow 'to have and to hold from this day forward, for better for worse, for richer for poorer, in sickness and in health, to love and to cherish, till death do us part, according to God's holy law'. And thereto she gave him her troth.

She actually took Philip Charles Arthur George as her wedded husband instead of Charles Philip Arthur George; but then he, holding the wedding ring on Diana's fingers, didn't pledge all his worldly goods to her as he should have done: he forgot the worldly and promised to share all her own goods, 'All thy goods with thee I share,' he said boldly. A moment later they turned to each other and giggled at their mistakes.

When they both said 'I will' and their promises rang out over the public address system into the streets of London outside, a great cheer went up which burst in through the sturdy stone walls and echoed through the quiet of the Cathedral. And when the Archbishop said 'I pronounce that they be man and wife together,' the cheers were louder still.

'Here is the stuff of which fairy-tales are made,' announced Dr Runcie at the beginning of his address, 'The Prince and Princess on their wedding day. But fairy-tales usually end at this point. . . . This is not the Christian view. Our faith sees the wedding day not as the place of arrival, but the place where the adventure really begins.'

Diana looked precisely as though she was setting out on an adventure as she curtsied to the Queen and walked down the aisle as the Princess of Wales. Her veil was now thrown back so that nothing hid the look of pure delight on her face. She walked with a firm hold of her Prince's right arm, her head held high, and smiled at the rows and rows of beaming faces in the congregation.

The majestic crashing and booming of Elgar's *Pomp and Circumstance* which carried them down the aisle – specially chosen, as Charles had explained, to be 'stirring, dramatic and noisy . . . because if you have something rather quiet, you can start hearing your ankles cricking' – gave way outside the Cathedral doors to an almighty roar from the crowds packed forty deep on either side of the waiting coaches.

There was a jubilant peal of bells from the north-west tower above them, a rich clang of the seventeen-ton bell, Great Paul, in the south-west tower, and suddenly church bells all over the City of London burst into music. The noise and the cheering remained with Charles and Diana as they sat smiling and waving in their open carriage all the way down Ludgate Hill, along Fleet Street, past the Law Courts, into the Strand, Trafalgar Square, into the Mall and back home to Buckingham Palace, past flags and flowers and faces filled with pleasure – old and young faces, black and white, and some even painted red, white and blue.

Champagne which had been cooling in the water around the Queen Victoria Monument spewed up into the air as they rolled in through the gates of the Palace, and there were still more cheers from members of the Household staff as they drove into the inner quadrangle.

The Queen and the rest of the wedding party followed five minutes later to more cheers; the Queen with Earl Spencer, the Duke of Edinburgh with Frances Shand Kydd, in traditional style, followed by the Queen Mother with Prince Andrew, and the remainder of the Royal Family in another five carriages behind.

When the last of the coaches was past, the crowds which had been lining the wedding route flocked like an insurgent army into the Mall and down towards the Palace in such numbers that there was barely a patch of the distinctive red road to be seen.

They had come for the balcony appearance, scheduled for about 1.15 p.m.; a solid, seething mass of patriotic hats and T-shirts and flag-fluttering humanity, packed tight against the Palace railings, began to chant: 'We want Di, we want Di, we want Di, we want Charlie.'

Inside the Palace official wedding party photographs were being organized in very little time and under great duress by Patrick Lichfield, the Queen's cousin. He was well used to such group photographs, where the family hadn't seen one another for ages and couldn't resist chattering, and had the brainwave of taking a whistle with him. It worked wonders and he was through the family groups in the forty minutes allotted to him, and on to the portraits of Charles and Diana alone.

Recorded for posterity, the bride and bridegroom's next duty was to the crowds who couldn't have waited a minute longer. The balcony doors opened and the Prince and Princess of Wales stepped out to an ear-splitting howl of delight from the people below. They were soon joined by the Queen and the rest of the immediate wedding party: the attendants, supporters, parents and grandmothers.

Diana smiled, waved and put her arm around one of the children for reassurance; the sight of so many hundreds and thousands of people in every direction as far as the eye could see must have been unnerving. But by the time she came back for the second time, she seemed more relaxed, and the more she came out the more natural she became. On the last appearance, the fourth in thirteen minutes, she bent her head for Charles to kiss her – the first time one member of the Royal Family has publicly kissed another on the balcony of Buckingham Palace – and the crowds went mad. They roared with delight, burst into song, cheered and shouted, waved and laughed, and they even kissed strangers.

After thirteen minutes, with the crowds still cheering and calling for more, the long glass windows to the balcony closed and Charles and Diana went inside to greet their guests – mostly relatives, plus the crowned heads of Europe present – for the wedding breakfast. One hundred and eighteen people were invited to the 'breakfast', a three-course lunch consisting of brill coated in lobster sauce, *supreme de volaille Princess de Galles*, and strawberries and cream, followed by wedding cake.

There were actually sixteen wedding cakes on display,

fifteen of which were unsolicited gifts. The official cake – enough to feed a thousand people – was a feat of culinary engineering. It was a five-foot, five-tiered, 255-lb hexagonal masterpiece, made by the Royal Navy Cookery School in Chatham. It had taken four men two days just to sort the fruit, and check each and every currant, sultana, raisin and cherry. The master baker, Chief Petty Officer David Avery, had spent eleven weeks creating the finished results, a tour through the tiers of the couple's lives, their coats of arms, family crests, and pictures of their homes painstakingly etched in colour on the white icing.

Charles cut the cake with his ceremonial sword, Andrew proposed a toast, Charles replied, and Diana had her first taste of navy rum, added to the wedding cake at her husband's special request.

Whether or not it was the navy rum at work, she and Charles came out on to the balcony again an hour later with the Queen and the Duke of Edinburgh for an unscheduled appearance, to the utter delight of the crowds who had stayed to see the couple go off on their honeymoon.

The bride and groom finally left the Palace for their honeymoon twenty minutes later than planned, in another open laudau, covered in rose petals and confetti, trailing blue and silver helium balloons, and with a 'Just Married' sign pinned to the back – the work of Andrew and Edward.

Diana had changed into a coral pink going-away suit designed by Belville Sassoon, with a matching hat with ostrich feathers made by the Knightsbridge milliner, John Boyd. The diamond earrings she had borrowed from her mother for the wedding had been replaced by large pearl earrings to match her new five-string pearl choker. She looked magnificent, and the crowds who lined the route from Buckingham Palace to Waterloo Station, where they were due to catch a train for Romsey, cheered and waved with unflagging enthusiasm.

The decision to spend most of their honeymoon on board *Britannia*, and to join it at Gibraltar, had been made some months before, but their plan to spend the first three days of it at Broadlands, the Mountbatten family home in Hampshire, now owned by Lord Mountbatten's grandson, Lord Romsey, wasn't announced until a week before the wedding.

The train was waiting for them on Platform 12 at Waterloo, but before climbing aboard, Diana suddenly stopped and kissed the two people who had been responsible for organizing the whole triumphant day: the Comptroller to the Queen, Sir 'Johnnie' Johnston, and the Lord Chamberlain, Lord Maclean, who said it was 'a lovely surprise'. Certainly not the sort of thing any other member of the Royal Family would have done: but then Diana is not going to be like any other member of the Royal Family.

Broadlands was an ideal place to have chosen for their first few days of marriage. Quite apart from Charles's own happy memories of the house from the days when his favourite 'Uncle Dickie' was alive, there was an element of superstition in the choice – his parents had begun their very happy marriage at Broadlands in 1947. It was also a magnificent house, set in six thousand acres of peaceful countryside with riding and salmon fishing in the River Test – not a totally selfless choice. Lord and Lady Romsey had moved out to give Charles and Diana the entire run of the place to themselves, and they spent two days away from the crowds, and three nights in a large four poster bed in the Portico Room, with splendid views across the grounds and the Test.

At the end of this short spell of peace and quiet Charles and Diana set out for the next part of their honeymoon. They were driven to Eastleigh Airport, twenty minutes away, for the flight to Gibraltar in an RAF Andover, with Charles at the controls.

Britannia had arrived in Gibraltar the day before, and the small British outpost on the tip of Spain, whose border with the mainland had been sealed off in 1969, was in a fever of excitement. The mile-and-a-half route to the docks from the airport, with its runway jutting dangerously into the sea, was festooned with flags and buntings, looking much the same as the streets that Diana and Charles had left behind in England, except that they had run short of Union Jacks on the Rock and had to use French flags which were, after all, the same colours. Crowds of thirty thousand – almost the entire population of the island – lined the road and cheered and waved until they were hoarse, and until Charles and Diana, who had been driven in an open Triumph Stag sports car, were safely aboard the royal yacht.

In the evening the Prince and Princess entertained the Governor and Lady Jackson, and a few local dignitaries, to drinks on board. Later that night they sailed out of Gibraltar towards the south-east, bound on a two-week magical mystery tour, followed but never sighted by their faithful friends from the press.

Buckingham Palace, which has always enjoyed playing a cat and mouse game with the press, was determined that on this occasion the honeymooners were going to be left in peace, and so they were. Rumours, whether planted or not, circulated like wildfire amongst the reporters, photographers and the television camera crews – not just from Britain but from all over the world – and they all set off like baying hounds in boats and aeroplanes hopping from one Greek island to the next, as one mention of a sighting followed hot on the heels of another. But no one ever knew the exact course of *Britannia* until she turned up for a pre-arranged stop-off at Port Said in Egypt twelve days later.

The success of it all was due to the careful planning by Prince Charles's private secretary, Edward Adeane, and his assistant private secretary, Francis Cornish, who had spent a lot of time leap-frogging ahead to the countries into whose waters they had plotted to sail, to seek their help with security.

Britannia's actual course, when she slipped out of Gibraltar under cover of darkness on 1 August, was to the Algerian coast, where she spent two days while Charles and Diana settled down to the sheer luxury of no cameras and no prying eyes. For the first time in months they were quite alone, or as alone as a royal couple ever can be.

Britannia is large, and has a crew to match. It is regularly manned by twenty-one naval officers and 256 men, excluding the personal staff that members of the Royal Family take on board with them. Charles and Diana didn't take many: they had a valet and a dresser, plus a private secretary and an equerry.

But in the privacy of the royal apartments, in the stern of the ship on the weather decks, they were alone. They spent their days out on deck, sunbathing, swimming off the side, windsurfing, and playing deck quoits on the games deck, as often as not with members of the crew.

The officers on board and half of the ratings change every two years, but the remainder of the ratings are attached to the royal yacht for the rest of their naval service, so a lot of them were old friends, who had known Charles since he was a child. Charles had actually sailed on *Britannia* during her maiden voyage in April 1954. After the Queen's coronation in June the year before, she and the Duke of Edinburgh had resumed the six-month tour of the Commonwealth that they had had to abandon with the sudden death of George VI in February 1952.

On this occasion, the Queen had planned to link up with *Britannia* at Tobruk on her way home and had promised Charles, then aged four and a half, and Anne, two, that they could sail out to meet her there.

And so Charles and Anne were taken down to Portsmouth by the Queen Mother, and entrusted to the crew, who had installed a sandpit, a slide, and a model of *Britannia* mounted on a pedal car frame on the deck.

From Algeria Diana and Charles sailed on along the coast of Tunisia, up to Sicily through the Straits of Messina, and arrived off the Greek island of Ithaka. They lazily soaked up the sun and swam by day, and in the evenings they went to parties that each of the various messes gave for them on board, returning the hospitality in their own rooms on other evenings or simply enjoying their own company: listening to music, watching television, reading or playing cards.

After leaving Ithaka, the yacht had spent Sunday, 9 August at Grabousa, a pin-prick of an island on the north-west point of Crete. The next day Diana and Charles had stopped briefly at the tiny island of Thira and gone ashore, while for the next two days they cruised around in the clear blue Aegean, passing close to Rhodes, and down through the Mediterranean to Port Said in Egypt, where they dropped anchor late in the afternoon of the 12th. At Port Said a flotilla of small boats came out to greet them, ships' sirens blared and crowds on the quayside cheered, all drowning *Britannia*'s Royal Marine Band struggling to be heard above it all.

In the evening, the Prince and Princess welcomed President Anwar Sadat and his wife Jihan aboard for dinner in the royal dining room. This was intended to be a formal occasion, but Diana and Jihan hit it off together and the evening was surprisingly relaxed. So relaxed, in fact, that when the Sadats went to the airport at Hurghada three days later to see them off, Diana took everyone by surprise by giving them both a farewell kiss. They were people she liked, with whom she had had fun, and she had gone through twenty years of her life saying goodbye to people she had enjoyed meeting with a kiss. For an Earl's daughter it was an expected gesture: for a royal it was unheard of, but it was her third farewell kiss in two weeks of marriage, and an indication of the way things will be done in the future.

After their dinner with the Sadats, Charles and Diana had set off in *Britannia* through the Suez Canal and into the Northern Red Sea for the last couple of days in the sun, and their last days alone. On the Saturday morning they left *Britannia* and flew from Hurghada to Lossiemouth in Scotland to join the rest of the Royal Family at Balmoral.

They came home to Britain to a tumultuous welcome. The next morning, at the tiny country church of Crathie, which is normally lucky to see ten people on a Sunday, a massive crowd of ten thousand people came to watch them attend Morning Service. They had all come to see Diana. Schoolchildren showered her with roses through the open window of her car, and young and old alike gazed in delight at her bronzed smiling face, muttering that just a glimpse of her had 'set them up for the week'.

Later that week Charles and Diana both agreed to be photographed in one session by television and newspaper men from all over the world, on the understanding that thereafter they would be left in peace during their weeks at Balmoral. There were no courtiers present to vet questions or to keep order. It was the most informal meeting many of the journalists remember ever having had with the Prince.

A transformation appeared to have come over both of them. Diana looked prettier than ever after her weeks in the sun – tanned, happy, relaxed and glowing. Charles looked years younger, far less as though he carried the weight of the world on his shoulders. He seemed unable to keep either his hands or his eyes off his bride. If his head had ruled his choice a year earlier, during his weeks at sea his heart had well and truly made up for lost time.

Diana declared their honeymoon had been 'fabulous', while Charles smiled triumphantly at the reporters and photographers who had failed to trail them and said provokingly: 'I hope you had a nice time going round the Mediterranean.' One pressman admitted it had been expensive, to which Charles replied, 'Good!' Diana was asked what she thought of married life. 'I can highly recommend it,' she said. 'It is a marvellous life and Balmoral is one of the best places in the world.'

But even the best place in the world can pall, and after two weeks at Balmoral, miles away from anywhere, without a sound to interrupt the peace and quiet, or a bright light to cheer the landscape, Diana was bored to distraction.

She was a country girl, to be sure, but she had always liked her country in small doses with plenty of good lively company which, kind, friendly and adoring as the Royal Family were, they didn't provide. And their preoccupation with dogs drove her mad.

Charles spent a lot of his time salmon fishing, which kept him for hour after hour thigh-deep in the River Dee. Diana had a go at it, but she wasn't totally hooked. She didn't have the temperament – she was much too impatient. Charles also spent a lot of time shooting, and although Diana could shoot and did from time to time, it wasn't her favourite way of spending a day. Horses left her cold. So there was nothing much else to do but walk over miles of beautiful, treeless, heather-clad grouse moor.

After two weeks Prince Andrew took the initiative and rang her old flatmates in London, inviting them up to Balmoral to keep Diana company. Virginia Pitman and Carolyn Pride both flew up, and provided a little light relief for a while. Diana also found Sarah Armstrong-Jones's arrival at Balmoral a blessing, and the two of them spent a lot of time together, leaving the rest of the family to their royal recreations, while they went off to Ballater in Diana's new Ford Escort to look at the shops, or slipped below stairs to chat to the staff.

There were more formal distractions from time to time too, like the Braemar Games which Diana enjoyed, although she rather blotted her copybook there by giggling and whispering to Charles during the National Anthem. The Queen gave her a hard stare and was not amused. But Diana was not squashed: she continued to enjoy herself, roared with laughter at the children's sack race, and was delighted with the Highland Fling, which was flung on the stage right in front of her.

More than a thousand of their presents had meanwhile been put on display at St James's Palace, insured for four million pounds, along with Diana's wedding dress and shoes, one of the bridesmaids' dresses and one page-boy outfit. Diana and Charles had received ten thousand presents in all, ranging from priceless sapphire and diamond jewellery from the Crown Prince of Saudi Arabia to a ribbon bag made by a ninety-six-year-old blind woman.

There were large quantities of glassware – bowls, decanters and vases – including a cut-glass bowl from Nancy Reagan which was said to have been worth forty thousand pounds; there were carpets and rugs, and gold and silver and porcelain. The Northern Ireland linen industry had given a traditional present of thirty pairs of double sheets, pillow-slips, satin-bound towels, face-cloths and handkerchiefs, all of which the Palace had specifically requested to be plain white. There were paintings and books, a microwave oven, a tea-maker, wooden clothes pegs, salt and pepper pots, soap, a pin cushion, a vacuum cleaner and a wind-surfer. In fact they had received just about everything that one could possibly think of, including two cows from the island of Jersey which, needless to say, did not go on display at St James's.

During the eight weeks that the presents were on show, more than two hundred thousand people filed into the state apartment at St James's Palace to see them, and most of those people had principally come to look at the wedding dress. They began queueing at 7 a.m. on most days, three hours before the doors opened, and the queue at any given time stretched halfway down the Mall towards Buckingham Palace. Some people waited for as long as five hours to see with their own eyes what Diana wore; they had come from all over the country, some had even come from the other side of the world.

Diana had provided the world with a fairy-tale come true. Her wedding may have been the most expensive recorded in British history, but it also raised more than £750,000 for charity by way of profits from the official programmes and souvenirs that were on sale, from the fireworks display held the night before, and from admission fees to the show of wedding presents in St James's Palace. It had also done immeasurable good to the morale of the country, to tourism, and to the security and popularity of the monarchy.

Prince Charles summed up his feelings about his wedding day three months later at a lunch in the Guildhall. 'We still cannot get over what happened that day. Neither of us can get over the atmosphere; it was electric, I felt, and so did my wife.

'I remember several occasions that were similar, with large crowds: the Coronation and the Jubilee, and various major national occasions. All of them were special in their own way but our wedding was quite extraordinary as far as we were concerned. It made us both extraordinarily proud to be British.'

PRINCESS OF WALES

THE WEDDING was just the beginning. Diana's popularity has continued to increase beyond everybody's wildest dreams, and not for any fairy-tale reasons. She is a real live princess who has proved herself to be all things to all people. She had gone out and met the public with a kind of freshness and friendliness which no member of the Royal Family has ever had. She has shown a rare sensitivity for ordinary people. She says and does whatever comes naturally at the time, whether it is admitting to feeling ghastly, or warming a frozen child's hand between hers.

Yet she has retained a distance. And for those who want their princess glamorous, they have it. Diana is worth going to see if only for the stunning clothes she wears, the hats, the shoes, the make-up and the jewellery. Queen Victoria once said, 'Dress is a trifling matter but it gives also the outward sign from which people in general can and often do judge upon the inward state of mind and feeling of a person.'

Never a truer word could have been spoken about Diana. Her clothes, from the expensive but unobtrusive tartan skirts and twinsets that she was wearing early in 1979 to the bright, bold and dramatic outfits she chooses for herself today, reflect a very positive growth in Diana's confidence and personality. In 1979 she was a seventeen-year-old girl from a broken home, with two sets of parents, no qualifications and an uncertain future. Today she is very nearly twenty-two, a wife, a mother and a Princess, loved by a Prince, adored by a nation, and with every expectation of a full and happy future.

There was great speculation as the weeks went past and the honeymoon at Balmoral continued, that Diana was being turned into a 'royal' up there in the heather, that she was being groomed and coached and put through her paces before being launched on 'the job'. However, when she finally did appear on her first tour of duty, a three-day visit to Wales in October, it was apparent that either the speculators had been wrong, or that Diana had proved an unwilling pupil. Charles had promised the Welsh people that once he was married he would bring his bride to Wales and so he did. And Diana set off into the crowds collecting armfuls of flowers and gifts, shaking hands and talking, noticing the old in wheelchairs and the young in arms, and winning hearts in a way no one could ever have taught her.

In three days the couple covered four hundred miles and every county in Wales. Travelling sometimes by royal train, where they spent their nights, and sometimes by glass-topped Rolls Royce, they visited seaside resorts, historic towns, country showgrounds, leisure centres, hospitals, mining communities and industrial cities. It was an awe-inspiring initiation. People turned out to see their Princess in their thousands, and to begin with Diana was clearly intimidated. Stepping out of the car or the train at each stop was like walking into a party full of total strangers and being told to mix. Diana had never been a very good party-goer at the best of times, but the knowledge that these people would treasure what she said and how she looked for the rest of their lives gave her a new kind of courage.

Prince Charles had once been asked whether he was able to pinpoint any particular moment when he realized that he had been born to be King. He replied, 'I didn't suddenly wake up in my pram one day and say "Yippee". I think it just dawns on you, slowly, that people are interested . . . and slowly you get the idea that you have a certain duty and responsibility. It's better that way, rather than someone suddenly telling you "You must do this" and "You must do that", because of who you are. It's one of those things you grow up in.'

But it was not one of those things Diana had grown up in. Suddenly someone *had* said 'You must do this' and 'You must do that' because of who you are. She had known all this, of course, before she agreed to marry Charles, but it wasn't something she gave very much thought to. She was just like every other hopelessly-in-love young bride who believes that marriage is the important thing and once she is married everything else will work out: love will conquer all.

She had been asked at the time of the engagement whether she found daunting the transition from nineteen-year-old nanny to someone who would in all probability become Queen. 'It is,' said Diana, 'but I've had a small run-up to it all in the last six months, and next to Prince Charles I can't go wrong. He's there with me.'

But Prince Charles won't always be there with her, and they hadn't even come to the end of their honeymoon before they were parted, and Diana was given her first taste of what life as Princess of Wales will really be like. In October their friend President Sadat, whom they had sat laughing with over dinner on board *Britannia* just two months earlier, whom she had kissed goodbye on the tarmac at Hurghada, was brutally gunned down by terrorists in the middle of a military parade in his own capital. Charles flew off to Cairo to attend the funeral, and although Diana wanted to go too, Buckingham Palace put its foot down: it was far too dangerous. The Egyptian renegade General Saadedin Shazli had made a statement in Libya that Egypt was 'unsafe for foreign dignitaries', and seven extra bodyguards flew out to Cairo on the plane with Charles. The funeral fortunately went without incident, but the whole business gave Diana food for thought.

There were threats of violence in Wales too. Fire bombs were found in an army recruiting office in Pontypridd and in the British Steel headquarters outside Cardiff, while anti-royalist demonstrators in Bangor and Swansea let off stink bombs and waved placards saying 'Go home, Diana' and 'Go home, English Prince'. A woman in Caernarfon sprayed the royal car with white paint; and Welsh Nationalists chanted slogans and waved banners in Carmarthen and Cardiff. The BBC were sent a letter, written in Welsh, warning 'We will not forget 1969 – beware Caernarfon', signed 'Rhys Gethin'. It was a name used by a small extremist group, *Meibion Glyndwr* (the Sons of Snowdonia), two of whom had been blown up in 1969 while planting a bomb intended for the train carrying Prince Charles to his investiture in the castle.

Security precautions were tight during the three-day visit of the Prince and Princess. Manhole covers and letter-boxes by the roadside were checked and sealed over the dozens of miles the couple drove by road between one stop and the next, and re-checked before the entourage set off. They were escorted front and back by police cars and police motorcyclists, and every road junction along the route had a uniformed policeman standing guard over it. When Charles and Diana were on walkabouts, there were marksmen on the rooftops, dog handlers on the ground and police everywhere – hundreds drafted in from other parts of the country to reinforce the local ranks. Before the party stopped at a town, Special Branch officers checked the guest lists of every hotel and boarding house in the area; and Charles and Diana's own personal bodyguards kept close, their eyes darting uneasily over the crowds. Not the slightest motion passed them by.

One journalist from *The Times*, Tim Jones, was almost locked up in the middle of the night. He had absent-mindedly brought his father-in-law's gun in the boot of his car, having first collected it from the gunsmiths where it was being repaired. Relaxing over a few drinks with colleagues in the bar of his hotel on the second night he mentioned the gun and said he thought he would bring it in from the car and put it in his room for safekeeping. At 2 o'clock in the morning he was woken out of a deep sleep by the noise of his door being virtually lifted off its hinges by the largest man he had ever seen in his life, from Special Branch, who interrogated him for the next three hours as to how he came to have a gun in his room.

But however vigilant everyone was, Diana knew perfectly well that if anyone was determined enough both she and Charles were sitting targets. It didn't seem to bother her. The response she got from the crowds, the vast majority of whom had come to love not protest, was so warm and enthusiastic that she seemed to put all thoughts of personal safety out of her mind. The crowds made it painfully obvious that they had come to see her, not Charles; and the more she realized it, the more confident she became.

'What nice shiny medals,' she said to one hunch-backed old

soldier at the Deeside Leisure Centre; and then to his beaming wife, 'Did you polish them for him?' She remarked that she hoped people would notice how patriotically dressed she was in green, white and poppy red, the colours of the Welsh flag; and when a seven-year-old boy in the crowd at Rhyl called out, 'My Dad says give us a kiss,' she smiled and responded, 'Well then you had better have one,' and leaning forward kissed him on his right cheek.

But she had chosen the patriotic outfit without much thought to the weather. Wales was bitterly cold those three days, and nowhere colder than inside the great grey granite ruins of Caernarfon Castle, where an icy wind from the sea howled round the battlements and froze hundreds of skimpily dressed children to the bone. They had been waiting for nearly two hours by the time the royal couple finally arrived and were met at the gates by Lord Snowdon, Constable of Caernarfon Castle – a familiar face at last, whom Diana promptly kissed.

Formalities over and the local dignitaries duly greeted, Diana eagerly set off ahead of Charles towards the waiting children, clasping her hat to stop the icy wind whipping it, shaking hands, stretching forward on tip-toe to reach people in the rows behind, bending down to be on the right level for the children, squatting for the smallest, smoothing their blue-cold faces, rubbing their shivering hands and obligingly wiggling her fingers to show off her engagement ring when asked for a peep.

In return she was given presents: flowers, sometimes just single stems, drawings, poems, candy, dolls, for which she sometimes said '*diolch yn fawr*' – Welsh for 'thank you very much'. In St David's, on the second day, she was given a Welsh doll and a moment later came upon a little girl dressed in national costume. 'I've got a smaller version of you here,' said Diana holding up her doll. The children told her they were off school for a week for half-term. 'That's a long time,' she said, looking cheated. 'I only used to get four days.' Everything she said was perfectly judged for the person she was addressing. It was a knack no one could have taught her in two years at Balmoral, far less two months. She was born with it. People who stood out in the pouring rain and the freezing cold for hours on end felt amply rewarded. As one enraptured woman at Rhydyfelin on the last day of the tour put it, 'Now I've seen her, she's everything I thought she would be. She's the flower in the royal forest.'

Charles was left apologizing for not having enough wives to go round on occasions when the crowds lined both sides of the street and he and Diana took one side each. Pleased as they were to talk to the Prince of Wales, they couldn't disguise their disappointment if their side got him rather than her. 'Do you want me to give those to her?' he asked as people looked longingly after Diana and held out offerings for her. 'I seem to do nothing but collect flowers these days,' he said. 'I know my role.' Sometimes he called out 'Diana love, over here,' to try to bring her across. He was obviously fiercely proud of his princess, and the more she walked about and heard her name called and met such enthusiasm, the more she grew to enjoy herself. As Prince Charles later said, the trip had been 'overwhelming. All that was entirely due to the effect my dear wife had had on everybody.'

Another person in the entourage round Wales who found that her role included collecting flowers was Anne Beckwith-Smith, Diana's newly appointed principal Lady in Waiting. Reminiscent of a Norland nanny, she hovered around while Diana loaded her arms with gifts that she had been given. Three Ladies in Waiting had been appointed for Diana, all of whom she had chosen herself, but from a short-list most probably drawn up by the Palace. All three were at least ten years older than her. Lavinia Baring and Hazel West, who are both married, were to be extra Ladies in Waiting, called upon only for Diana's public engagements. Anne Beckwith-Smith, on the other hand, began working at the Palace on a regular basis, helping with Diana's correspondence, running errands, making appointments and generally taking care of those areas of her life which didn't fall into the domain of Oliver Everett, her private secretary. His concern is principally the Princess's public life, although all three of them work very much as one.

The thirteenth-century castle at Caernarfon was a significant calling place in Charles and Diana's tour of Wales, particularly their brief, teeth-chattering appearance high up at the Queen's Gate balcony, known as Eleanor's Window, overlooking the town square. It was named after Edward I's Queen, whose son became the first English Prince of Wales in 1284. Two years earlier his father had conquered the country, killing the indigenous Prince, Llewelyn ap Gruffydd ap Llewelyn, more simply remembered as Llewelyn the Last, and embarked on one of the biggest and most costly castle-building projects in history – now the glory of Wales to all but a handful who still resent the English invasion. After Edward's son was born, he took the naked child and held him aloft at Eleanor's Window, presenting him to the Welsh as their Prince. 'See,' he is reputed to have said, 'he doesn't speak English!' He didn't speak Welsh either – he was so young, the poor creature couldn't speak any language at all.

Since then Princes of Wales have traditionally been presented to the Welsh by the monarch – as Charles was at his investiture in 1969 – and Diana's appearance at Eleanor's Window as his Princess produced roars of delight from the crowds in the square below. Inside the ruins, a large choir of primary school children sang rousing Welsh songs.

Their second day began in the flag-strewn seaside city of St David's on the extreme south-west tip of Wales, where at first light excited people had begun crowding into the square and along the short route that they would walk to the Cathedral. Charles and Diana were due to join in a service to celebrate the eight-hundredth anniversary of the Cathedral – named after the Principality's patron saint – situated at the bottom of thirty-nine steep steps, said to have been the inspiration for John Buchan's novel of the same name. Charles had been to the city before – Britain's smallest with a population of only fifteen hundred – but less formally, in the days when he was studying Welsh at Aberystwyth in 1969. Ever since then, Dai Crust, the local baker whose rolls the Prince had eaten, had been known locally as 'Upper Crust'. And that day, as Diana came out of the service in the Cathedral, the baker's wife stepped out of the crowd and presented her with a book of her recipes.

It had begun to pour with rain during the service, while the chosen few sat within and thousands more stood outside in the

158

churchyard and listened over the tannoy. By the time Charles
and Diana reached Carmarthen in the afternoon the rain had
become torrential. It was icy cold and the streets were awash,
but still the crowds were in place behind the barriers two hours
before the couple were due to arrive, packed more tightly than
sardines, and soaked to the skin. The water ran off people's
hair in rivulets, and most people had given up with umbrellas
and settled for a soaking. Even Diana lookd damp when the
royal party finally came into view. She was carrying a large
black umbrella, which didn't appear to have done much good:
the ostrich feathers on her hat had taken a dive and her hat was
limp and flat, her legs mud-spattered, and her coat was
beginning to look as though she had slept in it. But she was still
smiling, giggling even, and if anything, walking at a more
leisurely pace than she had in the dry, as if aware of the
discomforts people were suffering to see her and wanting to
make it worth their while.

The enthusiasm was incredible, and Diana responded
energetically despite her own increasingly obvious exhaustion.
Frozen to the marrow, she had included seven stops on her
first day; soaked to the skin, she had survived eight stops on
the second day, and just as she must have wanted nothing
more than a long hot bath and an early night she had had to get
into fresh finery for a gala concert in Swansea. On her last day,
there were another eight stops, and so many people lining the
roadside in the mining valleys in the south of Wales that she
didn't even have a chance to relax the smile from her face in
between stops.

The last day began in mid-Wales in the Brecon Hills,
magnificent in their autumn colours, at the Royal Welsh
Showground, normally filled with livestock, but on that day
crowded with about four thousand locals, farmers,
schoolchildren, girl guides and boy scouts. Charles and Diana
were presented with a seven-month-old Welsh heifer called
Sandra, with enormously long eyelashes and silky black curls,
and a black Welsh Mountain yearling ewe called Fedw Suis,
who as a breeder so delicately put it 'had had her chance', and
might have been pregnant.

Both animals, gleaming in the sunshine, all curls and horns

and eyelashes and firmly held by their handlers, cried out to be stroked or hugged or in some way appreciated, but Diana didn't feel compelled to do anything. She thanked the donors quite politely but she didn't touch either animals. She is no sentimentalist; heifers, sheep, pheasants, deer – they all live for farming or eating, and there's no point in petting or making a fuss over them, as you might a guinea-pig.

It was shortly before her tour of Wales that a story appeared in one of the popular papers that Diana had made an unclean kill while stag shooting during her honeymoon at Balmoral. There had been public outrage; typical letters to newspapers read, 'Princess Di is known for hanging her head shyly. She should now hang it in shame'. 'When Prince Charles married his lovely bride, I thought: here is a gentle, sensitive girl who will rise above our sad violent world. My illusion is shattered for good with one shot.' Others suggested coercion: 'I will never believe that gentle Di would ever willingly hurt an animal. What sort of pressures have been put on that poor girl?'

The fact is Diana didn't wound a stag; she killed it outright. Shooting is not her favourite pastime, but it is a skill she learnt at her father's knee – before his illness, Earl Spencer was regarded as one of the best shots in the country – and Diana is accomplished, like every other member of her family, who have been shooting with the Royal Family at Sandringham for years. Diana and Charles's first adult meeting was in the midst of a pheasant shoot, as were many of their subsequent meetings. Shooting is one of Charles's most pleasurable hobbies – which does yield a considerable income to the royal estates; and, not surprisingly, he spent his thirty-third birthday last November shooting on the van Cutsem's estate near Newmarket, and bagged six brace. When he can't shoot, he hunts, mostly he says because he enjoys the company. But the Royal Family are renowned as a blood-thirsty lot, and although Diana doesn't share her husband's passion for blood-sports, their philosophy is in tune.

One passion that they do share is children, and both had been far more demonstrative when looking at new-born babies in a hospital at Llwynypia in the Rhondda Valley than they had been appraising their new-found heifer that morning. Both were full of questions for the new mothers: Diana wanted to know how long they had been in labour, and how they managed to keep their babies quiet; but when asked when she and Charles intended starting a family, she just giggled and refused to be drawn. In fact she was two months pregnant at the time, although no one could have guessed. People might even have been excused for thinking that she had developed anorexia. She had lost a stone before the wedding, at least another stone since and appeared to have almost entirely lost her appetite.

The reason behind her loss of appetite became clear six days later, when on 5 November at 11 a.m., Buckingham Palace issued a formal announcement that the Princess of Wales was expecting a baby in June.

The Prince and Princess of Wales, the Queen and the Duke of Edinburgh and members of both families are delighted by the news [said the announcement]. The Queen was informed personally by the Prince and Princess.

The Princess is in excellent health. Her doctor during the pregnancy will be Mr George Pinker, Surgeon-Gynaecologist to the Queen.

The Princess hopes to continue to undertake some public engagements but regrets any disappointment which may be caused by any curtailment of her planned programme.

The baby will be second in line to the Throne.

The announcement might have sounded starched, but it was a vast improvement on the coy message that Buckingham Palace had put out on 4 June 1948, when the Queen had been pregnant for the first time, with Charles. 'Her Royal Highness,' it ran, 'the Princess Elizabeth, Duchess of Edinburgh, will undertake no public engagements after the end of June.'

Pregnancy was not a subject to be spoken about in public in 1948, and in fact there was still an archaic custom in existence that the Home Secretary of the day had to attend and verify each royal birth. The custom was said to have begun after 1688 when James II's Queen produced an heir for the Catholic Succession after years of miscarriages. This arrival was so

161

timely that many Protestants accused her of having the baby smuggled into her bed in a warming-pan. The baby, who grew up to be the Old Pretender, put paid to the political machinations of Diana's ancestor, Robert, the 2nd Earl of Sunderland, and sent him fleeing for his life to Holland.

At times over the centuries, it had proved an embarrassing custom. In 1841 Sir James Graham, the Home Secretary, had waited uneasily at one end of a large palace bedchamber, while Queen Victoria gave birth to the future Edward VII at the other. When it was all over, Sir James declared, 'I congratulate Your Majesty most warmly. A very fine boy, if I may say so.' Whereupon, from behind the heavy curtains of the four poster bed, an indignant voice replied: 'A very fine *Prince*, Sir James.'

Mercifully for both the present Queen, then Princess Elizabeth, and the Home Secretary, Mr James Chuter-Ede, George VI abolished the custom shortly before Prince Charles was born.

Diana was thrilled about being pregnant: to be married and to have a baby were, after all, her two greatest ambitions in life and she had achieved them both in a year. She rang up her close friends as soon as she could, to tell them before they read about it in the newspapers. People who have suggested that Diana will have to give up most of her friends now she is married under-estimate just how important they are to her. Throughout her life they have been one constant factor in an inconstant home situation and she has always relief heavily upon them for support and security. Where most people are careless, Diana has looked after her friendships: kept in close touch, in person, by letter or telephone. She doesn't see them so often now because her role as Princess of Wales keeps her too busy, but she still maintains contact wth them in other ways, and that won't change. She does, of course, still have far more in common with them than she will ever have with most of Charles's friends, the majority of whom are even older than he is.

Diana's world was looking up. Her Welsh tour had been a triumph, culminating in Cardiff City Hall where she was granted the Freedom of the City, only ever given to one woman before her, and that was the Queen. After the ceremony, she had delivered her first public speech, 'How proud I am to be Princess of such a wonderful place,' she had said with a simple sincerity, 'and of the Welsh, who are very special to me;' and then, to the delight of the hundreds and thousands of people who had cheered her round four hundred miles of their country, lapsed into Welsh to say: 'I hope to come here again soon.'

But after two days off Diana was back at work again, earning her palaces and her publicity, with a busy schedule: a concert at Blenheim Palace, and dinner with the Duke and Duchess of Marlborough; the opening of the twenty-fifth London Film Festival at the National Film Theatre; the pomp and pageantry of a State opening of Parliament; followed by a quick change to open an exhibition at the Victoria and Albert Museum. On the day of the announcement of her pregnancy, she accompanied Prince Charles to lunch at the Guildhall as guest of the Lord Mayor of London, Colonel Sir Ronald Gardner, while letters and telegrams of congratulations began pouring into Buckingham Palace and telephone calls from all over the world jammed the switchboard. William Hill, the bookmakers, were offering 10-11 on the royal baby being a boy, evens on a girl and 50-1 on twins, while Corals offered 4-5 on a boy, evens on a girl and 125-1 on twins. In no time at all dozens of lovingly knitted little woolly boots and bonnets began arriving by the sackful.

Diana's becoming pregnant straight after their marriage was just what both Diana and Charles wanted. The Prince was thirty-three that November and beginning to feel he had been missing out on something. But it was also a constitutional relief. There was no immediate danger to the monarchy, no republican forces whipping up emotion – not many people listen to Willie Hamilton – and even if a London bus were to flatten the Queen and Prince Charles on the same day, there would still be plenty of successors. But a direct heir is always preferable, and although Diana's youth means that there is plenty of time, Charles is a prime target for any trigger-happy, bomb-blasting lunatic, quite apart from the death-defying activities he goes in for voluntarily. It was plain that the sooner

Diana was safely with child the better; and although a great many people thought it sad that at twenty Diana would be tied down with children before she had ever had a chance to emerge as an individual in her own right, many more people were delighted.

Mr Hamilton, true to form, declared that his 'heart sank – it didn't take long to get the production line rolling, did it?' There was a possibility in those early months of her pregnancy that whatever 'came off the production line', as Mr Hamilton so poetically put it, might be second in line to the throne irrespective of its sex. A Succession Bill, introduced by Labour MP Michael English, would have done away with the existing law of primogeniture, under which it is always the eldest boy that inherits, whatever his position in the family; but the Bill failed to get through Parliament.

Diana had absolutely nothing to show for her two-month-old pregnancy on the Guy Fawkes Day when she lunched at the Guildhall, but she was so excited and so pleased to be able to come out into the open about her baby at last, that she couldn't resist wearing a great voluminous outfit.

But less than a week had passed before the grin had gone from her face and she was experiencing bad 'morning sickness' – something most women suffer to a varying degree in the first three months of pregnancy. As the name suggests, it's a feeling of nausea which is most commonly, but by no means always, felt in the mornings, often precipitated by the sight or smell of food, cigarette smoke, coffee or alcohol. Some women actually are sick and a lot feel faint. In addition almost every expectant mother becomes desperately tired in the early weeks – so tired that they can't eat or even smile. Diana turned out to be one of those women who got the lot with a vengeance.

As she confessed to a woman in the crowd in York, during a gruelling visit to northern England which had involved three walkabouts in one day: 'Some days I feel terrible. No one told me I would feel like I did.' She cancelled a lot of her engagements over the next few weeks, leaving Prince Charles to go alone to the Duchy of Cornwall and to Bristol, and to make apologies for Diana saying, 'You've all got wives, I'm sure you understand.'

The last Princess of Wales to have a baby was Princess May of Teck, wife of the future George V and Charles's great-grandmother, who gave birth to her sixth child, John, in 1905.

There have never been very many Princesses of Wales – in all the years since Edward I defeated Llewelyn and made his eldest son Prince of Wales in the thirteenth century, there have only been eight Princesses – Diana is the ninth – and of those eight only six ever had children while Princess. On the other hand, there have been twenty-one Princes of Wales, including Charles.

The first Princess of Wales was Joan, 'the Fair Maid of Kent', who married Edward, the Black Prince, in 1361 and produced two sons. Fortunately there was no call for Edward's bride to be 'without a past' in those days, or Joan would not have been the woman for the job. She was a widow when she married Edward, and had had a series of lovers before that, including the Prince's own father, Edward III. And it was she who provided the Order of the Garter, Europe's most ancient order of chivalry, with its famous motto. In the midst of a court ball, Edward III picked up Joan's garter and exclaimed to an audience of shocked and disgusted courtiers: '*Honi soit qui mal y pense*' – 'Evil to him who thinks evil.'

Neither the second nor third Princesses of Wales, Anne Neville and Catherine of Aragon, had children while Princess of Wales. Anne, daughter of Warwick 'The Kingmaker', had married Henry VI's son Edward when she was fourteen, but he was slain less than a year later on the field of Tewkesbury in 1471. She later became Richard III's Queen. Catherine of Aragon married Henry VII's son Arthur, in 1501, but her young bridegroom had also died less than a year later, and she subsequently married his younger brother when he ascended the throne as Henry VIII.

After Catherine there was no Princess of Wales for more than two hundred years. Caroline of Brandenburg-Ansbach became the next Princess in 1714, although she had already

165

been married for some time. Her father-in-law, George Louis, the Elector of Hanover, succeeded the childless Queen Anne in that year as George I and his son, her husband George Augustus, became Prince of Wales. They all came over to England together, although father and son soon fell out personally and politically, and the Prince and Princess of Wales set up a junior court in opposition at Leicester House in London. They had children both before and after Caroline was Princess of Wales, but the eldest, Frederick, aged seven when Queen Anne had died, was left behind and brought up in Hanover.

It was this Frederick, when he came to England to be made Prince of Wales after George I's death in 1727, to whom Sarah Duchess of Marlborough attempted to marry her favourite granddaughter, Lady Diana Spencer. The Prince had been more than willing, if only to escape from his parents, who in good Hanoverian tradition loathed him. 'My dear first-born,' Caroline declared, 'is the greatest ass and the greatest liar and the greatest canaille and the greatest beast in the whole world, and I heartily wish he were out of it!' Prime Minister Walpole quashed Sarah's wedding plans and instead it was Augusta of Saxe-Gotha, Frederick's parents' choice of wife, who became the fifth Princess of Wales in 1736. Augusta produced several children, including the future George III, but his children were the death of poor Frederick before he could ever become king himself. He was accidentally killed by a cricket ball, struck by one of his children: it hit and burst an abscess and he died of blood poisoning. On hearing the tragic news his father, George II, who was playing cards with his mistress at the time, simply said, '*Fritz ist todt*,' and went on playing.

Caroline of Brunswick became the sixth Princess of Wales when she married her cousin, the future George IV, Frederick's grandson. It was this Prince of Wales – all sixteen stone of him – who had been the lover of Georgiana Spencer, the Duchess of Devonshire, better known as 'the Duchess of Dimples'. When he first set eyes on Caroline of Brunswick, the day before they were married in 1795, the Prince turned to Lord Malmesbury, a diplomat who had been sent to escort his bride to London, and said: 'Harris, I am not well; pray get me a glass of brandy.' He drank copious amounts to get him through the marriage ceremony next day, and in later years Caroline told a friend: 'Judge what it is to have a drunken husband on one's wedding day, and one who spent the greater part of his bridal night under the grate, where he fell and I left him. . . . If anybody were to say to me at this moment, would you live your live over again or be killed, I would choose death.' They were formally separated soon after their only child, Princess Charlotte, was born in 1796.

The seventh Princess of Wales, Alexandra of Denmark, who married Queen Victoria's son Bertie, the future Edward VII, is the one to whom Diana has been most likened. The Queen had sent off her daughter Vicky, Crown Princess of Prussia, to scour Europe for a suitable wife for her brother, and she came up with Alexandra.

I never set eyes on a sweeter creature! [she reported]. She is lovely! Her voice, her walk, carriage and manner are perfect, she is one of the most lady-like and aristocratic looking people I ever saw! She is as simple and natural and unaffected as possible – and seems exceedingly well brought up . . . She does not seem the least aware of her beauty and is very unassuming. . . . You may go far before you find another princess like Alix.

Alexandra was seventeen when she first met Bertie in 1862, and she was warned to dress simply and not to smile as the Queen, still in mourning after the death of the Prince Consort the previous year, couldn't bear to see anyone looking happy. She and Prince Albert Edward became engaged that September, and until their wedding six months later Alexandra was obliged to stay with the Queen at Osborne and Windsor, to listen to endless stories about her late husband, 'her beloved Albert', and learn what was expected of her as Princess of Wales. Her mother, meanwhile, was not invited over from Denmark, and her father was put up in a hotel. But Victoria was delighted with her future daughter-in-law. 'She is so good, so simple, unaffected, frank, bright and cheerful, yet so quiet and gentle', she wrote in her diary. 'She is one of those sweet creatures who seem to come from the skies to help and bless poor mortals and lighten for a time their path.'

Bertie hadn't fallen in love with Alexandra at first sight, much to the fury of his sister, but she soon fell in love with him. As she told Vicky on their wedding day: 'You perhaps think that I am marrying your brother for his position. But if he was a cowboy I should love him just the same and marry no one else.'

Alexandra and Bertie were Prince and Princess of Wales for thirty-eight years together before Victoria died in 1901 and Bertie at last became Edward VII. During that time the Prince of Wales was given no constitutional power at all by his mother, and fell to women, drink and gambling, while his Princess stood tolerantly by. His Groom of the Stole in those years was the 5th Earl Spencer, the Red Earl, who on innumerable occasions tried to persuade Victoria to let her son replace him as a non-political Viceroy of Ireland. He pointed out that by taking up residence in Ireland, he would do far more to emphasize the monarchy's commitment to the country 'than any political measure'. After unsuccessfully pleading with the Queen for ten years, Spencer wrote to Victoria's secretary, 'I feel inclined to throw in the sponge and retire to my plough in Northamptonshire.'

By the time Bertie inherited the throne in 1901, his elder son Albert Victor, Duke of Clarence, known in the family as 'Eddy', was dead, so it was his second son, George, the future George V, who became Prince of Wales. His wife, the eighth Princess of Wales, was Princess May of Teck, like Diana a former pupil of West Heath. She had originally been engaged to Eddy, but he had died before their wedding and she had married his younger brother instead.

Princess May of Teck was Princess of Wales for only nine years, but Queen for a lot longer. She became Queen in 1910 when George V ascended the throne, and survived him by seventeen years, seeing two of her sons and one of her grandchildren inherit the Crown before her death in 1953 at the age of eighty-five. Throughout this period she provided a formidable example to all members of the Royal Family. Some of Charles's earliest memories are said to have been visiting her at Marlborough House, where he recalls meeting a dignified old lady, whom he called 'Gan Gan', sitting bolt upright, her legs on a footstool, surrounded by the array of precious objects that formed her famous collection.

Her interest and love of art, in all forms, were characteristics she had in common with Diana, her successor as Princess of Wales. The organizers of the Gonzaga Exhibition at the Victoria and Albert Museum had been very impressed by how much Diana obviously knew about art when she was shown over in November 1981. In other respects, Queen Mary and Diana have little in common, and Diana will prove a very different Princess of Wales. She will certainly be quite different in the way she brings up her children – different even from the way that the Queen or the Queen Mother have brought up their heirs to the throne.

The eighth Princess of Wales gave birth to her first child – the future Edward VIII – at White Lodge in the depths of Richmond Park. The Queen Mother gave birth to the Queen, then Princess Elizabeth of York, at her family home in Mayfair, 17 Bruton Street; and the Queen gave birth to Prince Charles, then Prince Charles of Edinburgh, in a makeshift surgery at Buckingham Palace. By choosing to go into the private Lindo Wing of St Mary's Hospital in Paddington to have William, Diana became the first royal mother to give birth to a direct heir to the throne in hospital.

The Queen Mother had her first child by Caesarian section which required a full anaesthetic, and the Queen also had an anaesthetic when she gave birth to Charles. Diana, on the other hand, was totally conscious for the birth of her baby, having had an epidural spinal injection anaesthetic, and Prince Charles was by her side throughout. He had indicated his intention to be there during their visit to Llwynypia Hospital on their Welsh tour. He had been chatting to a miner's wife who had given birth to a little girl just ten hours earlier, and whose husband had been with her throughout the birth. 'I think it's a very good thing for the husband to be present when a mother is having a baby,' the Prince said and then, turning to the press corps hanging on his every word, remarked, 'I expect I shall get a lot of letters about this.'

Queen Mary was a remote mother to her children, tending to regard them as additional and rather more tiresome items in her collection. She employed nannies, as was perfectly normal for a mother of her station, but it took three years of systematic ill-treatment of her two eldest sons before she realized what sort of nanny she had employed – and only then because the nanny had a nervous breakdown.

The Queen Mother, by contrast, adored her children and found it very hard to have to relegate them to the nursery, something that had never happened in her own family. She used to see them on every possible occasion throughout the day; but when Princess Elizabeth was just nine months old, her parents were sent off on a six-month tour of New Zealand and Australia. The Duchess found the parting almost unbearable, 'I felt very much leaving on Thursday,' she wrote to Queen Mary, who was sharing care of the Princess with her own parents, the Earl and Countess of Strathmore, 'The baby was so sweet playing with the buttons on Bertie's uniform that it quite broke me up.' When she came home six months later her baby daughter had cut her first four teeth.

The present Queen's call of duty was no less stringent. Like her mother, she too was delighted with her children, although of necessity less relaxed about nursery visiting hours. 'Don't you think he is quite adorable?' she wrote to a friend soon after Charles was born. 'I still can't believe he is really mine, but perhaps that happens to new parents. Anyway, this particular boy's parents couldn't be more proud of him. It's wonderful to think, isn't it, that his arrival could give a bit of happiness to so many people, besides ourselves, at this time?'

The Queen saw her children for half an hour at 9.30 every morning, and insisted whenever possible on bathing them herself in the evening. But she was frequently away: on a couple of occasions she went to join the Duke of Edinburgh, away on active service in the navy; she toured North America and Canada, missing Charles's third birthday, and went off on a Commonwealth tour soon afterwards; and after George VI's death in 1952 and her coronation the next year, she was forced to resume that Commonwealth tour and be away from her children for six months. The first time she ever heard Charles read was over the telephone.

Diana won't be content to visit her children for half an hour each morning and leave them for six months at a stretch. It was inevitable that she should employ someone to help her with them, who could take over when she has engagements, but it would never have been a professionally qualified, old-school nanny, like the ones who looked after the Queen's children. What Diana wanted was a mother's help, not a surrogate mother: someone qualified in much the same way as she was herself – by experience. And if she finds she has to go away on a long tour, she will simply take William with her.

She may have cancelled excursions to the Duchy of Cornwall and Bristol, but one engagement that Diana did keep was a visit to St Mary's Church of England First School in Tetbury before Christmas, where she joined in singing carols and turned down the offer of coffee with the staff, because 'that cuts down the amount of time I can spend with the children'.

Tetbury is the nearest town to Highgrove, the house in Gloucestershire that Charles bought from the Rt Hon. Maurice Macmillan, son of Harold Macmillan, in mid-1980, and where the Prince and Princess have said that they hope to spend four-fifths of their time in the next few years. Diana is keen that her children should grow up as naturally as is possible, and there seems to be a far better chance of that in the country than in Kensington Palace.

When Charles bought the house, the main attraction was the locality. As it is situated quite close to the M4 motorway, the house is within easy distance of London, Windsor and Wales, and provides an ideal springboard for the Duchy of Cornwall estates in Cornwall, Devon, Dorset, Gloucestershire, Somerset, Wiltshire and the Scilly Isles (where the Prince owns a three-bedroomed cottage, which he has seldom used in the past, but may well start living in now he has children).

There is hardly any shooting in Gloucestershire, but all his other pleasures are on hand; and Princess Anne lives just four or five miles across country at Gatcombe Park. Cirencester Park and Badminton are close for polo and horse trials, and there is racing at Cheltenham, Newbury, Bath and Chepstow. Best of all, Highgrove is right in the middle of the Beaufort Hunt country, far more so, in fact, than Badminton, the Duke of Beaufort's home where the hunt originates.

Although a much older house, Highgrove is reminiscent of Park House in a number of ways. There is a similar sweeping drive, views over parkland to one side of the house, woods to the other, and most of the garden laid to lawn, including a croquet lawn, with magnificent trees everywhere, planted by Colonel Mitchell who founded the arboretum at Westonbirt, and who bought Highgrove after the fire in 1893. There is good stabling – enough to accommodate ten horses – and three hundred and forty-eight acres of farmland, which in the Macmillans' day was used for dairy farming. There is also a walled vegetable garden, about a hundred and fifty yards from the house, which used to keep the whole family in food.

But Charles and Diana have inevitably changed a great deal both inside and out. The friends and relatives that came to the house in the Macmillans' day are now augmented by detectives equerries and secretaries who couldn't be expected to live as one of the family. So walls have been knocked down, doors resited, and the accommodation changed to suit the house's new needs. It is unlikely, however, that much space will have been devoted to offices. Charles has a study, but the majority of official work continues to be undertaken at Buckingham Palace, and both Charles's and Diana's private secretaries together with their other staff remain based in London.

In the garden, meanwhile, Diana and Charles have trimmed the giant cedar to let more light into the house, roses have been planted, and they have built up the wall surrounding the property and planted fast-growing trees to screen them from the road. They also have hung imposing new wrought-iron entrance gates, given to them as a wedding present by the people of Tetbury and made by a local craftsman.

Despite all this work, Highgrove does still have some major disadvantages. Even Maurice Macmillan, the house's previous owner, was surprised when Charles made the purchase, for he felt that Highgrove wasn't big or grand enough for the Prince. Most serious, it is a security nightmare, for there is a public right of way running through the garden no more than two or three hundred yards from the south side of the house – a footpath to the neighbouring village, used daily by about a dozen people on average. It would take an Act of Parliament to have that changed, so it may be that the Prince and Princess will be house-hunting again before too long.

Charles and Diana's other home is Kensington Palace, where their apartments were completely redecorated and refurbished. They have three reception rooms there, a dining room, three bedrooms, including a master suite, a nursery suite and rooms for the staff.

Kensington Palace was the home of William III and Queen Mary and the early Hanoverian monarchs, but when George III bought Buckingham House in 1762 and decided to turn it into a palace, he converted Kensington Palace into apartments for the Royal Family and grace and favour apartments for the royal household. Robert and Jane Fellowes, Diana's brother-in-law and sister, are therefore neighbours.

Before their Kensington Palace apartments were ready, Charles and Diana lived at Buckingham Palace, and actually spent far more time there than at Highgrove, even after they had officially moved in last October. Ironically, Diana could come and go far more freely in the crowds of London than in the quiet of the country. She was still the subject of enormous curiosity, particularly after the announcement that she was pregnant. The normally peaceful market town of Tetbury had become a tourist centre, and it was impossible to leave those splendid wrought-iron gates without the knowledge of half Fleet Street. Despite the security, a number of photographers with powerful telescopic lenses managed to take peeping-tom pictures of Diana at home. She began to feel as hounded and as trapped as she had done during the months that she was under siege at Coleherne Court – only this time she could see no end to it. During the previous year she had had no protection from Buckingham Palace: now she had the best they could offer, and she still had no privacy. The only escape would be to stay at home, never to do her own shopping, never to call in to see her friends, or be free to walk about like a normal person again.

The Queen came to her rescue and appealed to the media to lay off her daughter-in-law. She had taken this step once before in her reign, twenty-five years earlier, when Prince Charles first began school at Cheam in Surrey. The same

173

procedure was put in motion: the Queen's press secretary, then Richard Colville, now Michael Shea, invited the editors of all the national daily and Sunday newspapers, television and radio news, and the representatives of the Press Association, to a meeting at Buckingham Palace. The meeting concerning the Princess of Wales was held in early December with Christmas looming, and the Queen was doubtless prompted by the memory of the previous Christmas holiday at Sandringham, when the world's press had been camped outside the estate waiting for news of Diana, and had made it impossible for any member of the Royal Family to go anywhere without being followed and photographed.

Michael Shea put his case simply to the editors seated round a large table in a room on the ground floor overlooking the Palace gardens: Diana had not made any request herself, but was growing increasingly despondent about the idea that she could not go outside her own front door without being photographed. Moreover, there was considerable anxiety about the short-term strain on a girl of twenty, expecting her first child, who had not been subject to the public exposure since early childhood as other members of the Royal Family. It would be a tragedy, it was felt, if her present feeling of beleaguerment led to a change in the attitude that she and Charles held towards the press when they were playing an even more important role in the country. He appealed to the editors to consider regarding the private life of the Princess as 'private'.

Once Michael Shea had made it clear to the editor of the sensationalist *News of the World*, Barry Askew, that this did not mean Diana was on the point of having a miscarriage, but simply that the poor girl couldn't even buy a packet of wine gums without being front-page news, the group was ushered into an adjoining room for drinks with the Queen and Prince Andrew. The editors were generally agreed that the request was fair and it was an amicable meeting, but Barry Askew was brooding on the wine gums. If she had a craving for them, he said, she ought to send a servant out to fetch them. 'That,' said the Queen with a smile that cut to the quick, 'is the most pompous thing I've ever heard.'

The editors, with two notable exceptions, however, did respect the Palace's request, and the photographers were called off, although stories without pictures continue to document her life and scarcely a day passes without Diana's name appearing in at least one of the gossip columns. Meanwhile her public appearances were given maximum picture coverage, and nobody could be happier about this than the fashion industry.

As a traditional leader of fashion, this Prince of Wales has been a write-off, but his Princess is making up for his deficiency in her own clothes and may even in time brighten up her husband's dress, which has been described as a 'cult of studied shabbiness'. She has already persuaded him to have his hair cut by her own hairdresser, Kevin Shanley, to which he agreed, possibly to stop her attacking it again with her tapestry scissors as she did on their honeymoon.

But it is not only the Prince that she has influenced. Diana has been wearing three- and six-string pearl chokers which were once the fashion hall-mark of Princess Alexandra of Wales, but which have been out of favour for many years; and last Christmas the shops were full of them. Last summer there were runs on culottes, which she had worn on her honeymoon, and ethnic jumpers, like the one that she was photographed in at Balmoral; and high necklines and romantic ruffles have been in constant vogue in the shops now for nearly two and a half years. Diana is the toast of the rag-trade, and has done immeasurable good for British designers and the industry as a whole. If she didn't enjoy it so much, she could well have reiterated the views of the previous Prince of Wales, who once said that he wondered whether 'to certain sections of the press, I was not more of a glorified clothes-peg than the heir apparent'.

But however much good the Princess has done to British industry, a new outfit for every occasion – even bought at cost price – has had an effect on her husband's pocket. Charles very quickly announced that now he was married he would increase the amount he keeps of his income from the Duchy of Cornwall. The Duchy consists of 128,000 acres of prime agricultural land in the south-west of England, forty-five acres of valuable lettings in south London, the whole of the Scilly Isles and most of Dartmoor, all of which was set up seven hundred and fifty years ago to provide the wherewithal for the monarch's eldest son while he waits to become king. The first Duke of Cornwall was Edward III's eldest son, Edward, the Black Prince. In 1980 the wherewithal was not inconsiderable – £550,440 – and in the past Charles has given half of that to the Treasury in lieu of income tax. In future he will only give the Treasury a quarter, which will yield him roughly £8,000 a week to live on. Not a bad income for newly-weds. But he does have an extremely expensive lifestyle, and taking a wife has more than doubled it: he now has the added expense of staff for two houses, maintenance of Highgrove, Diana's personal staff, her wardrobe, her car. In the future there will be obstetric and hospital bills to pay, as well as baby clothes and equipment and, in time, school fees.

But all these are paltry compared with the enormous cost of performing public duties: the staff that he employs, the running costs of his office, transport, and presents to hand out to people that he visits. All these account for at least three-quarters of his total income from the Duchy.

Neither Diana nor Charles derive any income from the Civil List, unlike Princes of Wales in the past. For instance, Edward VII and George V, when Princes, not only took money from the Civil List but pocketed all the Duchy income as well. It was the previous Prince of Wales, the future Edward VIII, who began the custom of paying a portion of his income to the Treasury, but it is still a voluntary donation. The only call that could be made upon the Civil List is in the event of Diana being widowed before Charles inherits the throne. In that event she would be allotted a pension of £60,000 a year. But Diana is not totally without means herself. Thanks to her mother's guidance, the money she inherited from her great-grandmother, Frances Work, which was put into trust for her, was well invested in 60 Coleherne Court. The flat was sold shortly after her wedding, reputedly for £100,000 – double the amount she had paid for it two years earlier. Since then, the money has been invested.

But income from investments is all that the Princess will earn in the future. Her work will be purely voluntary, and she has already chosen five charities to which she has put her name, out of one hundred and fifty that asked for patronage. She has chosen the Welsh National Opera, the Royal School for the Blind, the Malcolm Sargent Cancer Fund for Children, the Pre-school Playgroups Association, and The Albany, a community centre in the East End of London. In addition, she will soon take on something involving the Duchy of Cornwall.

But conscientious as doubtless she will be, her job first and foremost in the coming years will be that of wife and mother. These have always come top in Diana's list of priorities; and when she is not on parade as Princess of Wales, she is just like any other well-to-do young wife. She and Charles argue from time to time, and like a great many women she was slightly eccentric while pregnant, but mostly she has carried on just as she always has. She wears off-the-peg clothes, drives herself around London, goes shopping, drops in to see her friends and has her hair done. The only difference is that she now has a policeman to accompany her. In the evenings, she and Charles go to the ballet or the opera, and the first anyone knows about it is when they look up from the auditorium at Covent Garden and see familiar faces in the Royal Box.

Diana has taken on 'the way of life – the job' that Charles once spoke about, on her own terms, but so subtly that not so much as a feather on a royal hat has been ruffled. She has 'finesse', that quality that Queen Mary once remarked had gone out of the world – 'that indescribable something which was *born* in one and which was inherited through generations'.

Her predecessor might not have approved of her kissing in public, wearing a bikini when six months pregnant, or nipping into shops like any member of the public to buy a romper suit or stock up with chocolate bars, but times have changed. The ninth Princess of Wales has brought the monarchy into line with the changes: she is a perfect blend of regal and real – the only sort of princess the British could have accepted in the 1980s. If nothing else, Queen Mary would most certainly have admired Diana's courage.

177

WIFE AND MOTHER

PRINCE WILLIAM of Wales was born weighing 7lb 1½oz at three minutes past nine on the evening of Monday 21 June, the longest day of the year, and as it happened one of the wettest. Diana had predicted that he would be born on her own, twenty-first, birthday but that was a ruse, a bit of mischief on her part to throw the press. Another 'exclusive' prediction by some newspapers also proved false, for the Prince was delivered not at Buckingham Palace, but in the private wing of one of London's top teaching hospitals, St Mary's, Paddington, where Princess Anne had had her two children, and where all royal babies had been born over the past eight years.

The Lindo Wing is an unpretentious-looking red-brick building, tucked behind the main body of the hospital in a side street, just a stone's throw from the busy goods yard of Paddington Main Line Station, and a ten-minute drive from Kensington Palace. Once it was learned that Diana had been driven there before dawn, people waited all day for news. They waited in the street outside, in the pouring rain, or they waited by their radios and television sets. It was to be a long wait.

The first person to hear news of the birth was the Queen, waiting on tenterhooks at Buckingham Palace with the champagne already on ice. She had spent the day at RAF Wittering, on official duty, but her mind was on other things.

By midnight the immediate members of both families had been told, including Princess Anne who was in America, and Prince Andrew who was still in the South Atlantic where he had been fighting with the Task Force in the Falkland Conflict. Prince Philip had been dining at St John's College,

Cambridge, and was just leaving for the Master's Lodge when he was called to the telephone. 'I hope it's good news?' asked his host as he returned. 'It's a boy,' said the Duke of Edinburgh, and gratefully downed a glass of brandy.

Princess Margaret was at the musical 'Song and Dance', and at the end of the show, dancer Wayne Sleep broke the news to a delighted audience. Prince Edward was told at Gordonstoun, where he was in the midst of 'A' level exams; while the Queen Mother heard the news at Clarence House.

Mrs Shand Kydd had arrived in London from Scotland the day before for the start of the Wimbledon fortnight, and having been telephoned from the hospital, she in turn phoned her mother, Ruth Lady Fermoy, her two other daughters, Jane and Sarah, and her son, Charles, also in the thick of exams at Eton. Diana's father was phoned by Prince Charles who sounded, according to Earl Spencer, 'absolutely over the moon'.

There had never actually been any question of Diana having her baby at Buckingham Palace – a story manufactured by the newspapers. The Queen, they said, was insistent that her grandchild should be born at the Palace, where she had been delivered of her own four children, but that Diana had preferred hospital. The two, so the story went, were arguing it out. The rumours persisted on and off for two months – despite denials from the Palace press office – with definitive pronouncements every now and again about who had won the battle.

All this was mere fantasy. Mr Pinker, Surgeon-Gynaecologist to the Queen, believes that hospital is the safest place, particularly for a first baby. Even though there would have been very little risk in a home delivery for someone as young and healthy as Diana, she herself would have been the last person to want to take it.

The Lindo Wing was chosen rather than any other hospital simply because St Mary's is Mr Pinker's home ground. He trained at St Mary's and has been a consultant gynaecologist and obstetrician there for the last twenty-four years. Since becoming the Queen's Surgeon-Gynaecologist in 1973, he has steered all expectant royal mothers that way. The Earl of Ulster, the Duchess of Gloucester's eldest child, was the first to be born there in October 1974, followed by his two sisters, Lady Davina and Lady Rose. Princess Anne followed suit in 1977, when she presented the Queen with her first grandchild, Master Peter Phillips, and was back again for the birth of her daughter Zara in 1981. Princess Michael of Kent's two children, Lord Frederick and Lady Gabriella, were also born in the Lindo Wing and, as with all the others, were delivered by George Pinker.

So, while none of them could have been called blasé about royalty, the nursing staff were certainly not thrown into confusion by the arrival of the Prince and Princess of Wales at 5 o'clock that Monday morning. Diana, then in the early stages of labour, was welcomed by Sister Stevens, a softly-spoken, no-nonsense woman, aptly from Wales.

The maternity section of the Lindo Wing is on the fourth and top floor, reached by a small, old-fashioned lift. There is room for eleven patients in small square rooms with polished cork floors and regulation iron bedsteads, designed for business, not comfort. The mothers give birth in these rooms, in an atmosphere that is as close as possible to a home delivery, and while everything is perfectly hygienic there is no great display of gowns and masks, which make women feel as though they are in for general surgery. Mr Pinker's philosophy is that birth is a natural process and should be treated as such; and under normal circumstances he will deliver babies in his shirt sleeves with a plastic apron over the top.

Diana was a remarkably good patient. She went through sixteen hours of labour quite cheerfully, with Charles by her side, having been well prepared over the previous months by Betty Parsons, the doyenne of ante-natal teachers.

Betty Parsons, who is coming up to seventy, is a nurse by training, but has been preparing expectant mums for childbirth for thirty years, and has taught over sixteen and a half thousand women in that time, all of whom speak of her as though she were some sort of fairy godmother. She chatters nineteen to the dozen, and is filled with all manner of wit and wisdom about life and death and human nature which she manages to weave into her nine weekly classes. These are held in a small mews house near Claridges, in a green-carpeted room, prettily furnished with cushions and paintings, where girls come and 'huff and puff' as she calls it, and soak up such philosophies as 'drop shoulders', and 'accept what you can't change'. They go away not just ready for every eventuality in the course of childbirth, but with an ability to cope with life.

Betty doesn't believe in being dogmatic about the way in which a woman has her baby. If she wants to be plugged into an epidural spinal anaesthetic from the first twinge of a contraction, then that is the woman's privilege and it will be the right decision for her. Her prime concern is that no woman should feel a failure, whatever happens; that they shouldn't feel there is a standard to keep up, that doing it one way is better than another, or that childbirth is always a magical, mystical experience. 'Balance,' she believes, 'is the secret of life,' and that is the lesson with which her pupils go home.

She also likes to bend the father's ear for a good three-and-a-half-hour session at some stage in his wife's pregnancy, and say things she thinks both need to hear in each other's presence: how exhausted his wife is going to be in the early weeks after having their baby, and how much support and help and understanding she is going to need. The father's presence at the birth is for them to decide, although Betty personally believes, as does George Pinker, that it is an excellent thing.

Charles needed no convincing from either Betty Parsons or Mr Pinker. He has long believed that a father should be there to help and support his wife in labour. He had said as much at the hospital that he and Diana visited in Llwynypia in the Rhondda Valley, during their tour of Wales the previous October. Scarcely eight hours earlier one of the women in the maternity ward had given birth to a little girl, and Charles specifically asked her whether her husband had been with her for the birth. Yes, she said, he had been up all night; at which Charles had declared his approval of the presence of fathers. The squad of reporters had busily noted his every word.

It was no secret that Charles had always had a very soft spot for children, but watching his own child come into the world was an experience which clearly bowled him over, and one about which he talks now with the zest, if not zeal, of the newly converted.

He emerged from the double doors of the Lindo Wing at 11 o'clock on the evening of 21 June, grinning from ear to ear, and happy for once to stand and chat to the reporters and crowds that had been patiently waiting in the rain all day. The atmosphere was electric. It was like the night before the wedding all over again. People were singing and cheering and popping champagne corks. Some had jumped on trains for London the minute they had heard that Diana had gone into hospital, others had taken the day off work, more had simply come in their lunch hour in the hope of hearing some news, and then come back again after office hours. Even nurses from the main section of the hospital came and joined the crowds when they came off duty. By the time Charles appeared there must have been about five hundred people packed into South Wharf Road. They had known for an hour that the baby had arrived: not through any giveaway at the hospital, but from the 10 o'clock news broadcast on innumerable radios that people had with them in the street. 'It's a boy!' the cry had gone up, 'It's a boy!' And people began singing 'For she's a jolly good fellow', and stirring rounds of 'Rule Britannia'.

Standing on the stone steps, Prince Charles said, 'I'm obviously relieved and delighted – sixteen hours is a long time to wait.' Then, with a puzzled, far-away look on his face, he added, 'It's rather a grown-up thing I find – rather a shock to the system.'

'How was the baby?' someone asked. 'He looks marvellous; fair, sort of blondish. He's not bad,' replied Charles and when asked if it looked like its father, said, 'It has the good fortune not to.'

'Yes, thank you, my wife is fine,' he responded to another enquiry, 'Very very good.' And what about names? 'We've thought of one or two,' he said, 'but there's a bit of an argument about it. We'll just have to wait and see.'

People were pushing in on him all the time to get a closer look and to hear what he was saying. Suddenly a woman lunged forward, flung her arms round him and kissed him firmly on the cheek, leaving a bright red smudge behind. It was the very thing everyone wanted to do, and the excited crowd burst into song. 'Nice one Charlie!' they chanted like a football crowd, 'Give us another one!'

'Bloody hell,' said Charles with a wry smile, 'Give us a chance.' And then after a moment's thought added, 'You ask my wife; I don't think she'd be too pleased just yet.' And as he bent down to get into the back of his waiting car, the smudge of lipstick still on his cheek, and the crowds more jubilant than ever, he requested, 'Now can someone ask them not to make too much noise when I've gone. Rest is badly needed in there.'

There were still more crowds gathered outside the gates of Buckingham Palace, including a self-appointed town crier, who was hoping to be heard above the noise of car horns, and general merriment. At 10.25 p.m. the official announcement had been posted on the gates in traditional style, just as the official announcement of Charles and Diana's engagement had appeared just sixteen months earlier. 'Her Royal Highness the Princess of Wales was today safely delivered of a son at 9.03 p.m. Her Royal Highness and her child are both doing well.' It was signed by Dr John Batten, head of the Queen's Medical Household, Dr Clive Roberts, the anaesthetist, Dr David Harvey, the royal paediatrician, and Mr George Pinker.

Her Royal Highness and baby were indeed doing well. Mothers are not automatically swamped with love for their new-born baby, irrespective of how much the baby was wanted. It sometimes takes a while to come, particularly if labour has been exceptionally gruelling or if the baby has been removed from the mother for one reason or another straight after the birth. But Diana's had not been; she was delighted with her son from the very instant he had 'cried lustily', as the Palace later described it. Her medical advisors also strongly believe that immediate contact after birth is vital in the bonding process between mother and child, and Diana would almost certainly have been given him to hold before the umbilical cord was cut.

Sixteen hours is not an excessively long wait for a first baby. She had had a straightforward labour and a normal delivery, most probably entirely painless in the last stages, thanks to an epidural injection which anaesthetizes the lower spine and hence the birth canal, but leaves the rest of the body unaffected. So, Diana would have had all the thrill of watching the crown of her baby's head and his body emerge, without any of the physical sensation to mar the experience.

She had no food or drink during the day, except the occasional sip of water, just in case a general anaesthetic had become necessary. Her first drink was a cup of tea when it was all over. Then she and Charles were left alone for a while with their new son, to examine him – like any other parents – and to check the number of fingers and toes, and to congratulate each other on their brilliance.

Despite Charles's pleas to the crowds for quiet outside, Diana couldn't actually hear any noise from the street at all. Her room was on the opposite side of the building. His concern was undoubtedly for the hapless mothers who had rooms overlooking the road, who hadn't had a moment's peace all day. The only disturbance Diana was likely to suffer that night was from Baby Wales, the name on labels round his wrist and ankle, who was now cleaned up, checked, weighed and dressed, and cosily installed in a regulation perspex hospital cot-on-wheels by the side of her bed.

Tuesday would have begun around dawn with a cup of tea, and an early morning feed for young Wales, followed by breakfast for Diana, and a soothing hot salt bath. There are no bathrooms en suite in the Lindo Wing, only wash-hand-basins, so Diana would have been helped to one down the corridor. Then refreshed and comfortable, with her baby peacefully asleep in his cot by her bedside, and with flowers on every available surface and telegrams draped over the bedstead, she was ready to show him off to her visitors.

Charles was the first to arrive, at 8.45 a.m., by which time the police had brought in some sturdy barricades to make sure the crowds, already gathered outside the entrance, kept their congratulations verbal after their demonstrative show of the previous night.

Mrs Shand Kydd, accompanied by Diana's sister Jane, arrived about half an hour later, and left saying, 'My grandson is everything his father said last night. He's a lovely baby. The

Princess looked radiant, absolutely radiant. There's a lot of happiness up there.'

The Queen was next in. She arrived with a small present in her hand shortly before 11 o'clock, and left twenty minutes later looking jubilant – every bit the proud grandmother. The last familiar face to come and go was one very moved grandfather, Earl Spencer, who came out through the doors saying, 'It's a lovely baby,' over and over again.

Prince Charles's verdict the morning after was that his son was 'looking a bit more human this morning'. Diana, he said, was 'very well and recovering her strength,' and the baby was 'in excellent form too, thank goodness'.

They were actually both in such good shape that to everyone's surprise they left hospital that very afternoon. Diana was anxious to go home. She had been shown how to bath the baby by this time, how to 'top and tail' him between baths, how to care for his navel, as well as dress him and change nappies, of course. And, although hospitals generally like a patient to stay in for at least forty-eight hours after delivery, Diana was going home to rather exceptional circumstances. In addition to daily visits from Mr Pinker and Dr Harvey, Secretary of the British Paediatric Association, who will be responsible for young Wales's progress in the future, Diana would have an experienced nurse living in for the first few weeks. Ann Wallace was no stranger to either royal mothers or babies, having looked after Peter and Zara Phillips for Princess Anne in her first few weeks out of hospital. All in all, Diana would be in very capable hands.

And so at 6 o'clock, as forecast by Michael Shea to the waiting crowds and television cameras an hour earlier, the royal trio appeared at the doors of the Lindo Wing, flanked by a farewell committee from the fourth floor. Charles was carrying the baby, wrapped securely in a white shawl. Diana, by his side, was dressed in the same green dress with white spots in which she had travelled to the hospital thirty-seven hours earlier. She looked worn and a little flushed, but obviously thrilled, and was happy to stand for a moment and smile at the crowds who had waited so faithfully and now cheered so proudly. Then she took the baby from Charles, climbed gingerly into the back seat of their waiting car, and they were away.

The telegrams and flowers and presents continued to pour in from all over the world. Diana simply couldn't have timed the birth day better. After weeks of dread, fear and uncertainty, with troops in the South Atlantic – fear felt not least of all by the Royal Family themselves with Prince Andrew in the thick of it – the Falklands crisis was over, and everyone was in the mood to celebrate.

Predictably, Willie Hamilton, MP, wasn't. The baby's future, he announced, was 'going to be one long story of nausea, deference, and Land of Hope and Glory rubbish for many years'. But not many people were interested in what he thought. Diana was once again on her pedestal, and the ripples of criticism that had drifted her way on and off over the previous months were gone.

One particular incident saddened even her most devoted fans. Diana, it was revealed across the centre pages of one daily newspaper, had been offered and had accepted an entire range of nursery furniture from a shop in North London called Welcome to the World. The owners spoke with great excitement about how they had sent the Princess their brochure when she announced she was expecting a baby and, to their amazement, they had a telephone call one day from a man at Buckingham Palace to say that the Princess had accepted. All the items she had chosen, including a golden pine four-poster cot, complete with canopy and frills, and matching sheets, cot bumpers and quilt, had been duly delivered to Highgrove.

Their life there was short-lived. The next news was that every last frill and bouncing mobile was on its way back to North London. The royal pair were apparently incensed that the owners of Welcome to the World should have sought publicity about the furniture. It is a time-honoured convention that people who have the privilege of donating merchandise to the Royal Family don't shoot their mouths off about it afterwards.

The decision to send it less-than-graciously back was not Diana's, but the entire episode inevitably reflected badly on her. It reflected badly on the whole Royal Family; and the Palace then set down some very clear-cut rules about when gifts would and would not be acceptable.

Diana aroused further disapproval on one of her last public engagements before the birth; this time it was something her advisors should have seen coming. In April she had opened a new Sony Picture Tube Plant in Mid-Glamorgan, and posed for the attendant press and television cameras wearing protective glasses and a cap supplied by her hosts with SONY emblazoned across the front. She thus gave a non-British company better free publicity than they could have bought themselves in ten years.

There were also some strong editorials when the newspapers learned that she and Charles had had a German kitchen installed at Highgrove: another gift, magnanimously accepted. But this time the donors wisely kept their lips sealed, and the kitchen lived on.

Then there were stories that Diana had sacked one of her bodyguards because he made her nervous, that she hated Highgrove and insisted on moving, had snubbed some of Charles's friends, and was beginning to throw her weight around. She was cracking up under the strain of it all. Eminent psychiatrists, who declined to be identified, agreed she was showing classic symptoms of nervous fatigue. Each story was as fantastic as the last: all part of what Michael Shea, the Queen's press secretary, describes as 'the myths and legends' that are written about the Royal Family – written safe in the knowledge that Buckingham Palace very rarely bites back.

But, for the moment, the criticism was past. Diana had produced a prince, second in line to the throne; a prince who, the genealogists declared, would be the most British since James I, and the most English since Elizabeth I. Baby Wales was 39 per cent English, 16 per cent Scottish, 6¼ per cent Irish, and 6¼ per cent American. The rest was German.

A week later he was given some names. He was to be William Arthur Philip Louis, and never, by any stretch of the imagination, Will, Willie or even Bill. His name would not be abbreviated in any way, we were officially informed. Diana and Charles had chosen the name, as the Prince explained to a group of servicemen wounded in the Falklands, whom he was visiting that day, because 'it's not a name that now exists in the immediate family'.

The last Prince William, Prince William of Gloucester, was tragically killed in an air crash in 1972. The last king to bear the name was William IV, the third son of George III, who succeeded to the throne in 1830 at the age of sixty-four. He was never a very great king: he made long boring speeches and as Lord High Admiral upset everyone by ordering promotions on the spur of the moment. History remembers him with fondness as The Sailor King or, rather unkindly, as Silly Billy.

The first King William was William the Conqueror, bastard son of the Duke of Normandy, who claimed the English throne as successor to Edward the Confessor, and defeated Harold II at the Battle of Hastings in 1066. It was he who ordered the famous Domesday Book, in which all the lands of England were registered so that he might know precisely what was due to him in tax. According to a Saxon chronicler of the time, the survey was so minute that 'there was not a single hide, nor one vintage of land, nor even, it is shame to tell though it seemed no shame to do, an ox or a cow, nor a swine was left that was not set down'.

His son, William II, was thoroughly unpopular and self-indulgent, and was killed, no one knows whether by accident or design, while out hunting in the New Forest in 1100, just thirteen years after coming to the throne.

The third King William, formerly Prince William of Orange, came to England with his wife Princess Mary as joint king and queen after the flight of her father, James II, in 1968. It was to this Willian that Diana's devious ancestor, Robert, 2nd Earl of Sunderland, made himself so indispensable after his flight to Holland in the same year.

History may have influenced Charles and Diana's decision, but the main reason for choosing the name William was that they both liked it. Arthur is one of Charles's names and was one that his grandfather, George VI, also had; Philip is his father's name, as well as another of his own; and Louis was undoubtedly a tribute to his beloved great-uncle, Earl Mountbatten.

There was, too, an obvious bias towards Charles's side of the family in the choice of godparents, who were also announced that day, 28 June. Only one came specifically from Diana's camp, and that was Natalia, the twenty-three-year-old Duchess of Westminster; although Diana did, of course, know, like and approve of the others. They were, Lady Susan Hussey, one of the Queen's Ladies in Waiting; Sir Laurens van der Post, the seventy-five-year-old South African explorer and writer whom Charles had first met years ago through his interest in anthropology, and who had been Charles and Diana's guest at Balmoral the previous year; and three relatives – Constantine, former King of the Hellenes, Lord Romsey, with whom Charles and Diana had been holidaying in Eleuthera at the beginning of the year, and Princess Alexandra, one of the most popular members of the Royal Family.

But Diana's old friends hadn't fallen by the wayside. In fact, she saw several of them the next week at a small dinner party given for her twenty-first birthday. If any old friends had been dropped, they were Charles's – people like Dale Tryon and Camilla Parker-Bowles.

Otherwise there were no great celebrations for Diana's birthday. A lot of presents and cards arrived at Kensington Palace, including some that were hand-delivered by thirty small children from the Inner London Pre-School Playgroups Association, one of the charities of which Diana had become patron. But it was a sad, mismanaged gesture. The children arrived clutching flowers, and paintings and cards they had made, and stood outside in the rain singing Happy Birthday, on the understanding that Diana was going to come and see them, and possibly even give them a preview of Prince William. But Diana didn't show. She was busy inside her apartment with members of her family who had come to wish her a happy birthday, and was quite unaware that the children were there. They were finally moved on by a kindly-enough policeman, but by this time, as well as being soaked, many of them were in tears.

They had to wait, like everyone else, for the first official photographs of Prince William, which were released on 29

189

July, Charles and Diana's first wedding anniversary. But again there were no public celebrations; and in keeping with tradition, the christening a week later was a family affair too, with only sixty guests, including the medical team who had helped bring William into the world.

Everything about the christening, timed to coincide with the Queen Mother's eighty-second birthday on 4 August, was traditional. The service was conducted by the Archbishop of Canterbury, Dr Runcie, in the Music Room at Buckingham Palace; using the Lily Font which was first used for Queen Victoria's eldest child in 1840. The Prince wore the same fine cream Honiton lace christening gown, that had first been worn by Victoria's second child, the future Edward VII. The ceremony began at midday, and afterwards there was a champagne lunch in the State Dining Room, and the christening cake, by tradition, was the top layer of Charles and Diana's own wedding cake.

William had travelled to the Palace with his nanny, Barbara Barnes, who had taken over from Ann Wallace, as planned, a couple of weeks earlier. Barbara had previously been working for Princess Margaret's friends, the Hon. Colin and Lady Anne Tennant, daughter of the Earl of Leicester and the girl to whom Johnnie Spencer was once supposed to have been engaged. Barbara had known Lady Anne since she was a child, living on the Earl of Leicester's estate at Holkham in Norfolk, where her father was a forest worker; and had been looking after the Tennant children, Christopher, fourteen, and twin daughters, Amy and May, eleven, for the past fifteen years. Now that the girls were going to boarding school the family no longer needed a full-time nanny, and so Barbara had been in search of a job at the very time when word filtered down the 'nanny grapevine' that Diana was looking for someone to help her with William. Barbara was the ideal person: she had had no formal training, never wore a uniform, liked children to call her by her first name, and above all had a sense of humour. Perfect credentials for the job.

But the job was still very much one of mother's help and not mother's stand-in. Diana wanted to feed William herself, and in addition do as much of the daily routine as she could manage, such as dressing and bathing him, and keeping him entertained between sleeps. Charles took a very active part too, and within hours of having his son home, was an accomplished nappy-changer. Both of them revel in the time they spend with him, but apart from a natural inclination they both recognize the importance of being there, of being involved parents – a view strongly reinforced by Dr Harvey – and they are determined that Prince William will not suffer as they both did in their early years: Charles from parents who were perforce away for months at a stretch; Diana from a home that was split down the middle.

Diana now has that solid security she always dreamed of. She has a beautiful baby and a loving husband. She has fulfilled her ambitions; the fairy-tale has come true. But she has done more. She has set an example: she has made those women who don't want to tread the feminist trail, but who want nothing more than to marry young and make a career of motherhood, feel unashamed to do so. She has put 'the family' back on the map; and even if she achieves nothing else in her life, she will have done more good in her twenty-one years than most people do in a lifetime.

HER ROYAL HIGHNESS PRINCESS DIANA OF WALES

Born Diana Frances Spencer,
1 July 1961 at 7.45 p.m. summer time: 6.45 p.n. G.M.T.
at Park House, Sandringham

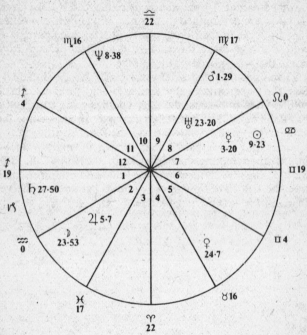

Siderial Time of Birth
06 · 37 · 12
06 · 45 · 00 GMT
12 · 82 · 12
13 · 22 · 12 Actual Siderial Time

The sun in Cancer gives Diana a quiet, reserved, retiring and sensitive disposition; yet she is inclined to publicity, changes of occupation and position, has a fertile imagination and loves nature and adventure. She is receptive and influenced by surroundings, industrious, prudent and very conscientious. She has a good memory, loves approbation, sympathy and kindness, fears ridicule and is greatly attached to home and family.

The Moon is the planetary sign, or ruler, of her sun sign, Cancer. It is in the 2nd house and in Aquarius: she is also therefore active, intuitive, agreeable, friendly and courteous. And she is sociable, sympathetic in manner, humane, independent and, on occasion, a little unconventional. Her inventive abilities are in the political, educational and scientific fields. She is interested in astrology. The Moon is in opposition to Uranus and in square to Venus. This indicates trouble from females or perhaps from her mother. However, Jupiter in the 2nd house helps to lighten or cancel out these two difficult aspects from the Moon. Jupiter's position also increases the chances of success, wealth and prosperity.

The combination of the Sun in Cancer and the Moon in Aquarius indicates skill in business enterprises, a love of intellectual pursuits and a personal charm which ensures popularity. She is extremely well balanced with great impartiality and clarity of judgement. She takes great care with regard to her speech, manners and appearance, and she has a strong aversion to extremes of any kind. Her ability to handle others is an important factor in her success with the public.

Diana's Saturn is in the 1st house, the house of which it is part ruler. This gives her dignity and the power to create the conditions that suit her. It also gives her power over enemies. Her Saturn makes no aspects and no detriments; it is just there to guide and help.

Mars, the traditional ruler of the 4th house, is in the 8th house, indicating gain from a legacy or estate.

Diana's Venus is in the 5th house, which it traditionally rules. This is a very fortunate placing, providing much pleasure, adventures, prosperous children and pleasure through them. It indicates a fruitful union producing beautiful children who may be endowed with artistic talent. The likelihood is that girls will predominate among Diana's children. Venus in the 5th house also denotes gain and success through love and friendship, the ability to entertain others and to enjoy success in music, dancing, singing, painting and in schools.

The Sun is in the 7th house and in trine to Neptune, a happy aspect made happier by Neptune's being in Scorpio, Charles's sign. This suggests a rise in life after or through marriage, a proud but magnanimous, warm-hearted partner, and a firm and lasting attachment producing much happiness. This placing of the Sun is good for partnership and for popularity with the public and with her elders.

Mercury is in the 7th house indicating that her partner will be shrewd, active, clever and progressive. The Moon is part ruler of the 7th house, bringing gain through marriage.

Uranus is in the 8th house, suggesting that great care must be taken with all children and with speculative ideas. Mercury, the ruler of the 8th house, is well aspected to Neptune in the 10th house, confirming the other indications of a good relationship with the public. Neptune is well aspected to the Sun, giving a highly inspirational nature, capable of attaining honour or position through some unique achievement. The ruler of the 10th house is Venus, suggesting that great care is needed with children's health and that there will be a gain through honours, sports or the stage.

Mars is ruler of the 11th house (the house of friends). It is well aspected to Mercury in the 7th house, bringing a loving partner with desirable friendships and social connections.

CHARLES AND DIANA TOGETHER

Both charts are in the Water duplicity and both have Fire signs rising. The Moons are sextile to each other which is a major indication of harmony. There is every opportunity for Charles and Diana to be very happy together, learning from and greatly helping each other; they were extremely lucky to find one another. Diana would be wise to listen carefully to Charles's advice on money matters, since he is more cautious than she is. There is a likelihood of twins among their three or more children.

HIS ROYAL HIGHNESS
PRINCE CHARLES PHILIP ARTHUR GEORGE
OF WALES

Born 14 November 1948 at 9.14 p.m. G.M.T.
at Buckingham Palace

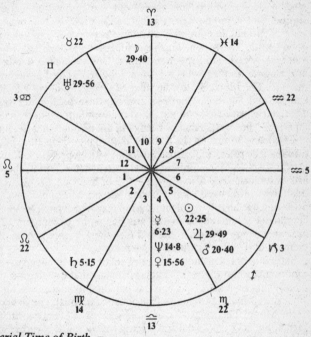

Sidereal Time of Birth
15 · 33 · 58
09 · 14 · 00   GMT
24 · 47 · 58
24 · 00 · 00
   47 · 58   Actual Sidereal Time

As Charles was born the Sun was rising over the Eastern horizon,
and was in Scorpio, indicating strength of character, dignity,

195

courage and determination. The Sun is in the 5th house which gives pleasure in places of amusement: Charles has great gifts, and had he not been born a Prince he could perhaps have topped the bill as an entertainer.

The Moon is in the last degrees of Aries, elevated in the 10th house mid-heaven, admirably aspected to Jupiter and in sextile to Uranus in the 11th house. Dynamic will power derived from this placing of the Moon will cancel out the opposition between Jupiter and Uranus. The Prince needs to watch extravagant friends. He has an extremely attractive personality and generally good health. The Moon, which is traditionally associated with the mother, is in trine to Jupiter and Mars. This indicates a strong but affectionate mother, who is both a good friend and a forthright mentor. The Moon is also the ruler of Cancer, Diana's sun sign. Cancer and Scorpio, Charles's sun sign, are both water signs. There is therefore a harmonious, sympathetic atmosphere in their marriage; they both gain knowledge of life through their feelings.

Charles's Venus is in Libra, the sign which this planet traditionally rules, and is in conjunction with Neptune; both are in good aspect to Mars. This suggests a great attraction to the fine arts and music, and also a great sense of humour. Problems are dealt with effectively and Charles has an admirable sense of priorities. He has plenty of vitality and staying power. The Venus-Neptune conjunction is in the 4th house, as is Mercury. This indicates some influence from his father; Prince Philip is a Gemini, and Gemini is ruled by Mercury.

Saturn in the 2nd house in semi-sextile to Mercury suggests caution in money matters. That is not to say that Charles is mean, merely that he is sensible about his personal finances.

Uranus is in the 11th house (the house of friends), and in sextile to the Moon. This makes for unusual and very clever friends. The 11th house is Uranus's natural placing which, taken together with this planet's helpful sextile to the Moon, lifts the disadvantage of its opposition to Jupiter.

The Ascendant is in Leo, the Royal sign. Leo is ruled by the Sun and therefore the Sun shares rulership of Charles's chart with Mars, the ruler of Scorpio.

Finally, a prediction: there will be at least three children in his life, because there are the following visitations: the Sun, Jupiter and Mars.

Born 21 June 1982 at 9.03 p.m. summer time: 8.03 p.m. G.M.T.
at St Mary's Hospital, Paddington

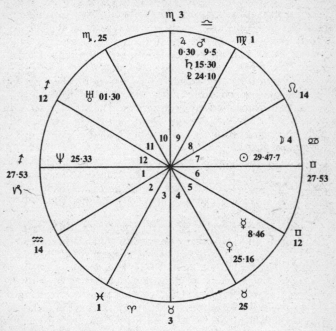

Siderial Time of Birth
05 · 57 · 25
08 · 03 · 00 GMT
14 · 00 · 25 Actual Siderial Time

**William's Sun is in Gemini and his Moon is in Cancer. This
suggests an emotional temperament, capable of deep feeling, but**

it may create restlessness and a dependence on others. His sensitivity will give him deep understanding, which in turn will make him tactful and diplomatic. Should he prove to be scientifically inclined, he is likely to exhibit a highly logical mind and an ability to expound complex arguments with great lucidity.

William's Sun is well aspected by Jupiter. Taken alone this would greatly add to William's chances of a successful life, rich in achievement. However, some less fortunate aspects to the Sun must also be taken into account, which suggest that William may experience some setbacks. Nonetheless, the Sun's aspect to Jupiter reveals a measure of good fortune because it indicates far-sightedness, a broad outlook and sound judgement.

The Moon is in semi-sextile to Venus, an excellent aspect: William will give and receive much affection, and display a kind, gentle, harmonious and happy disposition. The Moon is in the 7th house and in Cancer, his mother's sign. This will help to gain him popularity, success in all his dealings with the public and a rewarding social life.

The Sun being in the 7th house confirms what we might expect: that his marriage will be a matter of considerable importance, both to him and to others. His marriage partner is likely to be a person of exceptional loyalty and magnanimity, who will be popular with her elders.

Mars is in the 9th house, an interesting placing, which suggests that religion is likely to occupy a great deal of his attention: he will either be zealously religious, or antagonistic on philosophical grounds. His mental alertness will be stimulated by a love of change and he is likely to be extremely attracted by a roving existence. However, he must take care in strange surroundings.

His Mars in the 9th house is in trine to Mercury in the 5th house, meaning that his ability for rapid calculation and analysis enables him to sum up situations swiftly. Mars' placing in Libra is fortunate. It indicates amiability, charm, ardent affections, a love of beauty, and popularity.

Saturn is also in Libra. It reinforces the indications from Mars and adds other qualities to William's character: sweetness of disposition, a visionary outlook, spirituality, seriousness, tact, good judgement and a gift for getting on with his elders. Saturn's placing in the 9th house is a further indication of his interest in religion and philosophy and suggests strong orthodox opinions in this area. It also suggests a temperament appropriate to a royal

198

prince, and that he will hold an official position at the head of a college or institution. He is also likely to be very capable in judicial matters. However, this Saturn also reveals that some caution will be needed when he is travelling abroad.

Uranus is in Sagittarius, implying a highly-strung temperament, a strong intuitive faculty, an excellent imagination, liveliness and impatience with contradiction. Uranus is in the 11th house, the traditional House of Friends. His friends are likely, therefore, to come from advanced intellectual circles: their originality and creative thought will play a major part in moulding his personality. However, he must be very cautious of extreme ideas put forward by friends, who may not turn out to be friends in the long term. William is not himself a rebel, and will conform.

Neptune is in Sagittarius and in the 12th house, signifying happiness in quiet seclusion, but this can also indicate self-undoing, so he must beware of deception and fight a tendency to daydream, for there are goblins as well as fairies at the bottom of his garden.

Venus is in Taurus and in the 5th house, a fortunate placing indicating artistic gifts and an appreciation of music, dancing and the other arts. This also suggests that a happy married life and a deep attachment to children are likely.

Mercury is in Gemini and the 5th house, its own sign, and is in trine to Mars, one of the strongest indications of a bright and quick brain, great mental ability and shrewd, unbiased judgment. He will express himself well and have a talent for acting and other aspects of drama. This overrules the dreaminess derived from the placing of his Neptune; and also implies that his children will be beautiful.

With regard to his relationships with members of his family, he will undoubtedly get on well both with his elders and his peers. His Sun, being on the cusp of Gemini and Cancer, implies an especial bond of friendship and understanding with his grandfather, Prince Philip.

Astrological tables compiled by Frances L. Smith (Prince and Princess of Wales) and by Richard Mosly Smith (Prince William)

INDEX